A rare combination of humility, integri... God use this book to bring back spiritua... ...churches.

—CONRAD MBEWE, PASTOR, KABWATA BAPTIST CHURCH

My prayer is that this book will provide not only exposure but protection for people who might be drawn into error.

—JOHN MACARTHUR

A treasure trove for those wondering what to make of preachers who promise us health and wealth now, if only we will believe.

—MARK DEVER, PASTOR, CAPITOL HILL BAPTIST CHURCH

Teaches the biblical truth of the transforming grace of God in Christ that can change lives forever.

—H. B. CHARLES JR., PASTOR-TEACHER, SHILOH
METROPOLITAN BAPTIST CHURCH

A spine-chilling account of the author's escape from the dark world of the prosperity gospel to find the biblical truth.

—STEVEN J. LAWSON, PRESIDENT, ONEPASSION MINISTRIES

Graciously exegetes the prosperity gospel in a way that is clear and helpful to someone who is mostly ignorant of the movement.

—SUMMER JAEGER, PODCAST HOST, *SHEOLOGIANS*

We come away from this compulsively readable book as encouraged as we are enlightened. A testimony of grace that exalts the God who saves.

—OWEN STRACHAN, AUTHOR, *ALWAYS IN GOD'S HANDS*
AND *AWAKENING THE EVANGELICAL MIND*

Costi is a kind and gentle shepherd who loves his sheep. As you read this book, hear it delivered in the voice of someone who cares about you.

—TODD FRIEL, AUTHOR; HOST, *WRETCHED TV AND RADIO*

A refreshing and engaging reminder that the greatest blessing we could ever receive is already ours in Christ's gospel.

—JARED C. WILSON, ASSISTANT PROFESSOR, SPURGEON COLLEGE

This sobering assessment is also a loving and compassionate plea for those trapped in the prosperity gospel. I enthusiastically commend this book to you.

—Justin Peters, evangelist and apologist,
Justin Peters Ministries

Nothing short of an earth-shaking account of a man who once walked in darkness but has come into the light.

—Jeff Robinson, senior editor, The Gospel Coalition

Not only diagnoses the disease of the false gospel that has infested the church but also offers the cure.

—Dr. Richard Bargas, executive
director, IFCA International

Paints a picture of the prosperity gospel rarely seen. A clear account of the true gospel of Jesus Christ.

—Dawain Atkinson, host and founder,
The B.A.R. Podcast Network

A helpful primer on the prosperity gospel. The perfect blend of testimony, teaching, and tried-and-true tips for ministering to those caught in unbiblical teaching.

—Michelle Lesley, women's discipleship
blogger, author, and speaker

Costi has wonderfully laid out his story of being saved from the prosperity gospel world. I pray that this book will be widely read.

—Brooks Buser, president, Radius International

Eye opening, God honoring, biblically accurate, honest, and gracious. Required reading for every Christian.

—Barry L. Cameron, pastor, Crossroads Christian Church

Writing with raw honesty and without personal vendetta, Costi provides an enormous service to the church.

—Cory M. Marsh, assistant professor,
Southern California Seminary

GOD,
GREED,
AND THE
(PROSPERITY)
GOSPEL

GOD, GREED, AND THE (PROSPERITY) GOSPEL

HOW TRUTH OVERWHELMS
A LIFE BUILT ON LIES

COSTI W. HINN

ZONDERVAN
BOOKS

ZONDERVAN BOOKS

God, Greed, and the (Prosperity) Gospel
Copyright © 2019 by Costi Hinn

Published in Grand Rapids, Michigan, by Zondervan. Zondervan is a registered trademark of The Zondervan Corporation, L.L.C., a wholly owned subsidary of HarperCollins Christian Publishing, Inc.

Requests for information should be addressed to customercare@harpercollins.com.

Zondervan titles may be purchased in bulk for educational, business, fundraising, or sales promotional use. For information, please email SpecialMarkets@Zondervan.com.

ISBN 978-0-310-35527-4 (softcover)
ISBN 978-0-310-35529-8 (audio)
ISBN 978-0-310-35528-1 (ebook)

Scripture quotations, unless otherwise indicated, are taken from New American Standard Bible®. Copyright © 1960, 1962, 1963, 1968, 1971, 1972, 1973, 1975, 1977, 1995 by The Lockman Foundation. Used by permission. (www.Lockman.org)

Scripture quotations marked KJV are taken from the King James Version. Public domain.

Any internet addresses (websites, blogs, etc.) and telephone numbers in this book are offered as a resource. They are not intended in any way to be or imply an endorsement by Zondervan, nor does Zondervan vouch for the content of these sites and numbers for the life of this book.

Published in association with the literary agency of Wolgemuth & Associates, Inc.

Cover design: Studio Gearbox
Cover illustrations: vkilikov / Nikolay Antonov / Shutterstock
Interior design: Denise Froehlich

Printed in the United States of America

HB 04.08.2024

Dedicated to my wife, Christyne, and our children. This book is a "memorial stone" of God's undeserved grace upon us. May we always determine to be nothing but humble, faithful, trustworthy servants of the body of Christ. God gets the glory. We get the joy.

Statement of Financial Accountability

In an effort to operate with transparency and integrity, allow me to state the obvious: *a book speaking against the prosperity gospel technically makes money off of the prosperity gospel.* As such, it is my conviction that a word concerning the use of royalties is appropriate here. I intend to use proceeds from this book to fund theological education and resources for pastors and leaders who have been exploited by the prosperity gospel. I pray that this project will give more than it ever takes. May it be blessed to be a blessing.

Contents

Acknowledgments

A project like this is no solo effort. I've had tremendous support from people who have walked with me along the way.

I am grateful for my wife, Christyne. She's stood faithfully by my side, been a constant prayer warrior, and loved me unconditionally in my seasons of doubt and despair. She is the greatest teammate God could have ever given me. Her keen and constructively critical eye has been an asset throughout this project, and her willingness to sacrifice our one day off a week allowed me to write outside of my regular schedule working for our church. I didn't write this book on church time, when people expected me to be doing my job. She saw the big picture and believed this would be worth the sacrifice. She is my crown jewel (Prov. 12:4).

Next, I wouldn't be where I am today without our church family. The elders and members at Mission Bible Church have prayed for us, supported us, and encouraged us every step of the way. I'm thankful for the teaching pastor, Anthony Wood, who gave me my first "non-prosperity gospel" ministry job, then discipled me. Before I ever started seminary, he gave me three generations of theological books—my first library—from his grandfather (Ralph), who was a pastor, his dad (Gene), who was a pastor, and his own collection. These allowed me to learn historical truths that orthodox Christians have trusted for millennia. I owe a debt of gratitude to the Wood family for their selfless sacrifice for more than seven years.

Myriad friends have helped this project come to fruition. It was Dr. Owen Strachan, my friend and a professor from Midwestern Baptist Theological Seminary, who called me one sunny California afternoon and warmly demanded, "You have to write a book and help people on this topic!" I'm thankful for his passion for the truth. Erik Wolgemuth has become a trusted ally, and without his expertise and guidance, this project would not have come this far. Most of all, he prioritizes the gospel. I can't imagine partnering with anyone else to publish books. My editor, Carolyn McCready, and the entire team at Zondervan are heroic for being willing to stand up to the prosperity gospel and publish this book. Their guidance has been nothing but superb. With so much corruption in the world today, this generation needs a publisher like "Z" to put out material that rescues and inspires us to have hope.

I also want to thank you, the reader. You've taken a chance in buying the book, and for that, I am grateful. I don't know what expectations—or possibly burdens—you have in reading it, but I trust that God will inspire you through the pages that follow.

Mostly, I am thankful to my Lord and Savior, Jesus Christ, for saving my life. I was on a course of sordid gain and exploitation until he reached down and plucked me out of the misery I thought was living a dream. I have decided to follow Jesus. No turning back, no turning back.

Preface

The Heart of the Author

If sinners be damned, at least let them leap to
Hell over our dead bodies. And if they perish,
let them perish with our arms wrapped about
their knees, imploring them to stay. If Hell
must be filled, let it be filled in the teeth of our
exertions, and let not one go unwarned and
unprayed for.

—CHARLES SPURGEON

Just a short while ago, I had the chance to sit with one of my living heroes. Dr. Steven J. Lawson probably wouldn't like my choice of words because he doesn't view himself as heroic. But his advice rings in my ears every time I share the story of how I left the prosperity gospel.

"Telling your testimony is fine," he explained. "Paul the apostle did it. Many others have told their testimonies too. It can be helpful. But don't be one of those people who makes sin look so good that people want to go out and do it!"

His voice elevated with passion. "And it needs to point to Christ and glorify God! Storytelling for the sake of storytelling doesn't do much good. The gospel must be the focus."

My face flushed, my head bowed low, and my collar suddenly felt way too tight. At that moment, I resolved in my heart, *This prosperity gospel book needs to be inspiring. It needs to be truthful. But above all else, it needs to glorify God and communicate the gospel.*

This book is written with that purpose in mind. The glory of God is the chief end of every Christian's story. Those who have been redeemed tell of the Redeemer and warn of the dangerous distractions that lead to darkness. This may be my story, but its purpose is way bigger than me. I am sharing intimate details about the life that I was saved from so you too can be saved or help save others. Even then, it's not my story that will save you. Only the true gospel has that power (Rom. 1:16). This, ultimately, is a story about the one who can break any soul free from the bondage of deception. It is about the God of grace whose purposes and plans are unstoppable and who mercifully accepted me even after I had smeared his name for greedy gain. This book is about the mandate of the church to be salt and light throughout the earth and to stand up for the truth when Jesus Christ is being falsely represented as a commodity. There is much work to be done. God can, and does, save even the most ardent sinner. He also uses people to make a difference. Will you be ready when he chooses to use you in his plan of salvation? Maybe it's you who needs to change. Or maybe it's you who will help others to change.

As we journey through these pages together, I promise to be brutally honest. Although I will be naming names and calling out sin, I'll remain biblical in that approach. You may be a Christian who has been upset by the injustice of prosperity preachers, and you've picked up this book looking for answers. If so, I promise to provide answers to your most pressing questions.

Here are a few more things you should know:

I'm writing to the average reader. I've written in magazines, posted numerous blogs, and coauthored academically researched work geared toward Christians who know a fair amount about their faith. But this book is not going to contain endless chapters on the historical and theological roots of prosperity theology. Nor will you find hundreds of footnotes for academic works that I've used to back up each statement. Better authors and scholars have written textbooks on this topic, and I highly recommend one of those if you're looking to go down every historical rabbit hole of this dangerous belief system. Instead, I've written my story with biblical teaching points along the way to help you understand the truth.

Constructive critics have come to my table from both sides of the equation. Some have told me, "Costi, this book needs to be more theological. Stories don't save people." Others argue, "Costi, people being deceived don't understand theology. You need to relate to them with just your personal stories." The truth is, there is theology in this book, and there are stories. But neither side will be fully satisfied, which is why we'll always need more books on the topics at hand.

I'm on a rescue operation. There are millions of people who need to be saved from the prosperity gospel deception like I was. I'm trying to reach them, while at the same time inspiring other people to reach them too. I want people to see that the prosperity gospel is damning and abusive. It exploits the poor and ruins the lives of some of the world's most vulnerable people. This book is exactly what I would say if a confused prosperity gospel follower came to my house and sat with my wife and me at the kitchen table for several hours or if a curious Christian asked me, "So why did you walk away from that life?" It's also what I would say if someone came asking how they can make a difference. You'll find out what life is like in the prosperity gospel world, how I got out, and how you can help other people get out.

I'm not angry at my family. I love the Hinn clan with all my heart. My father is an affectionate, generous, and loving man. My mother is a hospitable, caring, and loyal woman. Like every family, we've had our challenges and disagreements, but all my life they've done nothing but try their best to love me as a son. My sisters are incredible women who would rush to my aid at the sight of a distressing text message. Every one of my uncles and aunts has treated me like their own since I was born. My uncle Benny always favored me, was generous beyond measure, and has never once insulted me to my face even in the midst of my opposition to the theology he has propagated.

Let me repeat what I've already said in a different way. This book is not a smear campaign or a vengeful crusade. This book is not about vendettas. It is about the truth. It is about loyalty to Jesus Christ and the true gospel. It cannot be overlooked, however, that a public stand for the gospel will not be without controversy and pain. Some relationships in the family have been strained because certain family members refuse to walk in the truth. No matter the cost, the true gospel is always more important than people pleasing.

I'm not judging anyone's salvation or final destination. This book is not a judgment concerning the souls of those caught up in the deception of the prosperity gospel or who preach it. As long as they're still breathing, anyone can repent of their sins and be changed by God's power. No doubt there will be people who say, "Who are you to judge someone else? Focus on yourself. Only God can judge." To them I refer to the words of Jesus and the apostle Paul.

Jesus warned the hypocritical Pharisees, "Do not judge so that you will not be judged. For in the way you judge, you will be judged; and by your standard of measure, it will be measured to you" (Matt. 7:1–2).[1] The plain meaning of the text is exactly what it says: how you judge is how you will be judged. If we apply that to this book, it means that if I am preaching the prosperity gospel yet calling it out at the same time, I am a hypocrite. If I ever go back to preaching the prosperity gospel, I should (and will) be judged in the same way that I am judging those who preach it. Jesus warned the Pharisees not to judge because they were judging with a hypocritical spirit—that's a dangerous way to go. It's one thing to be a sinner who turns from sin (we all should). It's another thing to be calling out the sins of others while you're still doing the very thing you're calling out.

Second, when Paul was dealing with an immoral situation in a church, he explained that judging inside the church is part of how we keep each other accountable. He writes, "For what have I to do with judging outsiders? Do you not judge those who are within the church? But those who are outside, God judges. REMOVE THE WICKED MAN FROM AMONG YOURSELVES" (1 Cor. 5:12–13). God will

---

1   The following article provides a deeper look at the topic of judging in relation to this passage and others, like Luke 6:37. Biblically speaking, we do need to analyze the teachings of all pastors (Acts 17:11) and compare them with Scripture. A verdict on their teaching doesn't mean a verdict on their souls. See Jeremiah Johnson, "Frequently Abused Verses: Is Judgment Always Forbidden?" https://www.gty.org/library/blog/B150916/frequently-abused-verses-is-judgement-always-forbidden.

have the final say on those who preach the prosperity gospel, and the Bible makes it clear that it won't be pretty. For now, we are called to speak the truth, protect people from harm, and pray for their souls. That's love.

I'm hoping you will do something about this gospel injustice. Without apology, this book is a call to action. Whether you identify as a non-Christian but believe in moral justice, or you are a Christian who needs to stand against this false gospel, I want you to be inspired to action. Every one of us has been blessed with a sphere of influence, and we have the power to use it to help others. It doesn't take much if we all do our part. Some of us need to speak up about the issue and be content with the controversy it brings. Others need to wake up and realize there is an issue. The prosperity gospel often slips under the radar, and in many places it is ignored as some fringe religion. But you know what? It's mainstream, and it's hurting a lot of people both inside and outside the church today. Millions of sick and poor people are being targeted in the third world by "pastors." Real pastors must be willing to stand for truth, and people must demand that they tell the truth. From major media to small country churches, let's do our part.

This deception is nothing new. Even in the early church, there were those who sought to distort Christianity and twist the gospel for personal gain. False teaching has always been a go-to strategy by the devil to confuse people and distort the gospel of Christ (Gal. 1:8). Let's not be surprised by this. But even more, don't let this be just another book on a challenge the church is facing. Let's join the ranks of those who long before us were faithful to stand up for truth and do something about it. I'm cheering you on, and I stand with you in this battle for truth.

So are you ready? Come with me into the depths of the

prosperity gospel and see for yourself whether it's a gift from God that can make us all rich or a weapon for greed mongers and charlatans. Walk with me on the fine line between truth and error and see what destruction looms and what great mercy lies in the hand of God. There is much to learn.

Let me tell you about God, greed, and the prosperity gospel.

1

Growing Up Hinn

I'm a sample of Jesus. I'm a super being.
—BENNY HINN

"Costi! Get over here now!"

With a jolt, I quickly turned to look behind me. I was in the green room at the healing crusade, mere inches away from the bowl of Cheez-Its, with plans to devour them by the handful. But instead, I was busted. It was my father hollering at me, and he was worked up into a frenzy.

"Oral Roberts is about to leave, and he is waiting to lay hands on you! What are you doing back here? The power of God is about to hit the place! Hurry!" he commanded. As we rushed down the stadium hallway, the scolding continued. "This is a once in a lifetime opportunity to be prayed for by the greatest man of God to ever live besides your uncle. Don't let me catch you back there again!"

I was just an awkward teenager enjoying a free vacation and trying to get a snack during the four-hour healing service that my uncle, Benny Hinn, was conducting, but my dad had other plans. It wasn't easy to endure the whole service without sneaking into the green room available for staff members. The people in there were always so nice that I preferred to be back there much more than in the arena filled with singing, yelling, fundraising, and commands to pray in tongues.

Everyone who worked the crusade as staff or volunteer always walked on eggshells during the service. If even attenders were caught moving during key points, it wasn't uncommon for my uncle to scold the crowd, "Don't move! Shhh . . . The Holy Spirit is here. Don't grieve him!" If a staff member or volunteer was caught—that was not pretty. No matter how long the service, you never wanted to get caught moving around and being a distraction, because we believed that Satan used distractions to cause people to miss out on their healing or their touch from God. Not paying attention? Jesus will simply pass you by.

This night, I had sneaked off the left side of the stage. Uncle Benny turned his head to speak to the right side of the arena, and I was out of my seat so fast nobody knew I had even been there. *Nothing can come between me and the green room now.* Or so I thought.

What I remember after getting busted is my father sobbing harder than I'd ever seen anyone sob as a frail old televangelist put his massive hand on my head and mumbled something about favor, anointing, the miraculous, and blessings. Then it was done. *Okay!* I thought. *Now that this is over, let's get back to the green room.* As I walked back to the arena floor with my father, he told me that the greatness of the moment I had just experienced would become evident in the years ahead. The special anointing on my life was set, sealed, and certain to produce abundant blessings. I was going to be a very healthy, wealthy, and happy man. *Bring it on, Lord, I'm ready when you are!*

Family Ties

While the Hinn name has come to be associated with healing services and the prosperity gospel, it wasn't always that way. The prosperity gospel and faith-healing belief systems represent only a few individuals within the entire family, and our family is huge. Many members of the Hinn family went a completely different direction in life. Even today, there are hardworking, God-honoring Hinns who have integrity in all they do. Some run successful businesses and work for major corporations. Some have worked in high-level positions with local government and US homeland security. Others have donated hundreds of thousands of dollars to the poor, expecting nothing in return. Most have never made a dollar they didn't honestly earn—most. Unfortunately, our family has not been in the news primarily for earning an honest wage or helping the poor. If you're reading this, chances are you've probably come to know the Hinn name for all the wrong reasons.

My father grew up in Jaffa, Israel. Arabic was the family's first language, and a small but loving home was the center of family life and happiness. My Greek grandfather, Costandi (Costi) Hinn, whom I am named after, worked a job for a department of local government and was well respected. False claims have been made about his being the mayor of Jaffa; he wasn't. My Armenian grandmother, Clemance Hinn, was a homemaker who could put you in a food coma for days. She was the most loving woman and a devoted mother, and even up until her death in

2016, her doors were open to everyone (as long as they stayed to eat!). The religious beliefs of the Hinn family were staunchly Greek Orthodox, though it was more cultural than anything. I visited the neighborhood my father grew up in as a young boy, and to this day people there tell stories about the warmth and love within the Hinn family home. But not every child in the Hinn home felt that love.

At around six foot two and 200 pounds, my grandfather Costi had a solid work ethic, a blue-collar outlook on life, and the looks of Clark Gable. He was a man's man. He expected his six boys to behave like men, and especially for his oldest son to possess some level of fortitude to establish himself as a respectable man. This is normal in Middle Eastern culture. At the very least, the oldest son is expected to make his father proud. He doesn't have to be rich. He doesn't have to be famous. He just has to do something respectable.

This expectation proved problematic for my uncle Benny, because he was withdrawn and stuttered, was much more feminine than the other boys, and made wild claims that were considered silly schoolboy tales. One of his most well-known claims was that when he was eleven years old, Jesus physically appeared to him in his room and revealed to him that he would be in ministry one day.

My grandfather Costi, however, was not impressed with Benny, his oldest son. Costi would say to him, "Out of all my children, Toufik [his real name is Toufik Benedictus Hinn], you won't make it." This crushed Benny's young heart. He would think, *Yes, I will make it!* To this day, my uncle Benny has made it clear that his father's words wounded him and motivated his desire for success in life. At the root of all of this family drama lies one thing:

a father who wanted his son to work hard and make an honest wage, and a son who felt rejected by his father and set out to prove him wrong.

War, Peace, and Poverty

In 1967, the Six-Day War erupted, and the Arab-Israeli conflict surged to new heights. So many bombs exploded near the Hinn family home that they frequently had to take shelter in underground bunkers. In a wise and protective move, my grandfather Costi found a sponsor in North America, and by July 1968, the family—Costi, Clemance, and their children—emigrated to Toronto, Canada. They had finally escaped the violence of the Middle East, but new challenges arose. Culture shock set in, and life would never be the same.

As the family settled into their new Canadian home in Toronto, Ontario, it became clear that life in the Great White North was not going to be like life in Israel. They spoke no English, had few friends, and were crammed into a small home. My grandfather went from steady work in Jaffa to a factory job in Toronto that paid modestly, and when another child was born, he had eight mouths to feed. The Hinn family experienced what many immigrants do. They figured out quickly that they would have to fight to survive.

My father and uncles were enrolled in school, where they quickly became a laughingstock. Because they spoke very little English, they used the word hi as a primary response. "Hello," someone would say. "Hi," was their simple reply. "What is your name?" the person would ask. "Hi . . . hi . . . hi," they would answer and quickly exit the scene. Many times they were bullied and made fun of for their ethnicity, so strength in numbers meant survival.

After fighting through the first few years, the young Middle Eastern immigrants found meaningful friendships with other immigrant children and settled into their peer groups. All of the brothers, that is, except Benny, who eventually was approached by a group of students at Georges Vanier Secondary School who wanted him to come to a prayer meeting. Perhaps seeking acceptance, Benny went to the meeting, where the students began to speak in tongues. Around the time that he joined the group and believed he was converted to Christianity, he began to claim having visions of Jesus.

The rest of the Hinn family was not happy about it. My grandfather made one thing very clear to Benny: "We did not come to Canada for religion. We came for peace." The religion of the Hinn family was already set. We were a Greek Orthodox family. This extreme version of westernized Christianity that Benny had just converted to was not going to fly.

Benny, however, continued down his path, determined to make something of himself. It didn't take long for him to find his calling. While the rest of the family pursued various jobs and education to establish a steady income, his greatest inspiration for a career came from an unlikely source: a woman preacher.

The Lady in the White Dress

The year was 1973. It was a cold winter Friday in Pittsburgh, Pennsylvania, just a few days before Christmas—December 21, to be exact. My uncle Benny's friend Jim had told him about a woman who he said was the most anointed preacher he'd ever seen. She had immense power and a flair for the dramatic. His curiosity piqued, Benny went along. Being young in his beliefs and without much grounding or sound teaching, he was ready for his next spiritual experience. What transpired inside the doors of First Presbyterian in Pittsburgh that morning changed the course of Hinn family history forever.

As Benny waited outside the church for almost two hours, he began to shake uncontrollably, like he did whenever he felt like God was touching him. Finally, the doors opened, and he and Jim rushed down the aisle and found seats. The worship continued until finally the world-famous faith healer named Kathryn Kuhlman (1907–1976) emerged at the crescendo of the music. Clothed in a flowing white dress, she captivated the audience with testimonies of healings and exciting teachings that seemed to be way beyond what an average Christian would experience. Time and time again, she pointed in Benny's direction and shouted, "Don't grieve the Holy Spirit!" Feeling as though she were talking directly to him, Benny hung on her every word as she taught things about the Holy Spirit that he had never heard before.

After the service ended and the crowd left, Benny stayed in the pew for quite some time and pondered what he had just witnessed. Then, back home in Toronto, over the course of a year, he felt God's presence visiting with him in his room, preparing him for his special ministry. Every day during that time, he woke up and said, "Good morning, Holy Spirit," a phrase that later became the title of his bestselling 1990 book.[1]

---

1   *Good Morning, Holy Spirit* was the vehicle for numerous false teachings about the Holy Spirit and the Trinity, teachings that confused Christians and non-Christians alike. Thomas Nelson, his publisher, reprinted the book in a second edition with many of the heretical teachings changed and corrected after evangelical theologians sounded the alarm.

The Birth of a Ministry

After seeing Kathryn Kuhlman in 1973, Benny Hinn knew what he wanted to do for the rest of his life.[2] He spent several years doing itinerate ministry, and at the same time, my grandparents softened to Christianity's message. They both surrendered their lives to Christ. My grandfather remained quite reserved in his faith, never speaking in tongues or engaging in any type of excessive beliefs and behaviors. My grandmother became somewhat more expressive in her faith but also kept her rudder deeply set in the Scriptures. Like any parent, they both loved Benny and did their best to be more accepting of his ministry path, but they were still extremely skeptical of his choice of friends and ministry circles. My grandmother Clemance often scolded him when he ministered with men and women who were known to be scandalous. In all the years of his ministry, no one was more critical and vocal about his alliances than my grandmother.

Eventually, Benny moved from Canada to the US and married Suzanne Harthern. During those early years, the rest of the family made professions of the Christian faith as well. In 1982, the family was shaken to the core by the death of my grandfather, and soon the rest of the family moved to the US, settling in Orlando, Florida. By 1983, Benny had founded the Orlando Christian Center, and three of his brothers joined him in pursuing church vocations. He built the church by pairing Bible teaching (with his special views added) with a healing ministry (using Kathryn Kuhlman's methods). It was the perfect formula for drawing a

---

2 For more on the Kuhlman-Hinn connection, see Benny Hinn, *Kathryn Kuhlman: Her Spiritual Legacy and Its Impact on My Life* (Nashville: Thomas Nelson, 1998).

spiritually curious crowd along with those who were desperate for answers and healing.

The ministry grew quickly, and thousands filled the seats of the church in Orlando. My uncles William and Sam, along with my father, Henry, were all groomed under Benny's ministry, and faith healing became the calling card of the Hinn family ministry. The brother who worked with Benny the longest throughout the years and revered him the most was my father. That's how I got so close to the center of the action.

The Hinn Family Franchise

As my uncle learned his craft from Kathryn Kuhlman, he also started adopting the health and wealth theology of prosperity preachers like Oral Roberts. My father followed closely in Benny's footsteps. After a few years of working for Benny at Orlando Christian Center, he took the same ministry model and planted a new church in Vancouver, British Columbia. Like franchising a business, with a brand customized for its location, Vancouver Christian Center was poised to be a hit.

The church launched with a bang in 1987, when I was three years old. Right from the get-go, it proved to be the right place and the right time for a church like ours. The Hinn name had grown more prominent in the Pentecostal and charismatic circles we were a part of, so the seats filled and momentum grew quickly.

A few years later, my father founded a school to teach everyday people how to do the miracles that Jesus did. He called it The Signs and Wonders School of Ministry. Anyone could pay tuition to learn how to do miracles, speak in tongues, and perform healings. He taught the classes and included historical material designed to inspire people to emulate the giants of the past. Teachings from people like John G. Lake (1870–1935), Smith Wigglesworth (1859–1947), Oral Roberts (1918–2009), William Branham (1909–1965), and Kenneth Hagin (1917–2003) were featured.

Vancouver Christian Center was loud and proud about its doctrinal foundations, and the Kuhlman-Roberts combination of teachings proved to be a cash cow. There was no subtlety about the direction the church was heading. Crowds came and money poured in. We began living the dream.

By 1997, when I was thirteen and the church was a decade old, our main home was a six-bedroom, eight-bathroom mansion that covered just a little less than ten thousand square feet in South Surrey, British Columbia. We had a private gate, a swimming pool, an indoor hot tub, a steam room, a sport court, and more than two acres of land to play on. My bedroom suite, larger than most people's living rooms, boasted a large walk-in closet, a bathroom with a Jacuzzi tub, standup shower, marble tile, and, yes, gold fixtures. We drove multiple Mercedes-Benz vehicles (from a convertible to an SUV), vacationed around the world, and stayed in expensive hotels. I remember celebrating my eighth birthday in the Holy Land (Israel) and riding camels as part of the celebration. Our family ministry trips to London, Paris, Maui, and everywhere in between were filled with privately arranged meetings to pray for and speak a blessing over celebrities, government leaders, and professional athletes from the NBA, MLB, and NFL. Wherever we went, our spiritual power lured people of prominence to something that could help them be more successful too. This all resulted in our getting to enjoy whatever luxury we wanted.

Signs, wonders, miracles, and prosperity preaching gave us a life my father only dreamed about as a kid. In our family, we truly lived what we believed. We were living the abundant, blessed life.

With an increasing global reputation attached to the family name, my father had succeeded in giving us the life he never had growing up in Israel, something he often told us was his goal. Meanwhile, Uncle Benny had officially proven my grandfather wrong. Benny had made something of himself. He was now living the life of the rich and famous. And I had come along for the ride.

2

Anointed and Arrogant

If I want to believe God for a $65 million dollar plane, you cannot stop me.
—CREFLO DOLLAR

"Just open up your mouth! Say whatever is on the tip of your tongue . . . just say, 'Ba-da-na-ta-ba-da-na-ta,'" an altar worker coached me.

I had been sitting in the youth section during a church service, and at the end of the service, my dad called the teens up to receive the gift of tongues. While the Bible describes the gift of tongues as the supernatural ability to speak in a real foreign language, we taught that it was the ability to speak ecstatic utterances that made no sense on earth but were understood in heaven. The rest of the congregation stood and stretched their hands toward us as altar workers made their way toward the front to pray with us.

"Lift up your hands!" my father exhorted. "Pray out loud in the Spirit!"

Having heard all of our parents speak in tongues, we knew exactly what my father wanted us to do. This was our rite of passage moment. It was time to get the gift of tongues.

Now the altar worker, a woman, issued more commands. "Don't think too much about it or you'll start to doubt and lose faith! Disengage your mind, engage your spirit. Shut yourself to questioning and open yourself to the flow of the Spirit. Lift up your hands and receive it!" Beside her, other altar workers and parents were praying and laying hands on the teens as they tried to impart whatever power they could to help us along.

I slowly mumbled my own words. Some of the kids just kept saying ta-ta-ta-ta-ta-ta to try to pass for tongue-talkers and escape the altar, but I managed to blurt out a bit more. Shekundalabakasho. Shekundalabakasho. I started to get louder. Maybe this is it? I thought. I didn't know whether it was supposed to be continuous language, but my tongue kept repeating, so I figured that had to be the way it was.

"You've got it! You've got it! There's the gift!" the altar workers affirmed as they continued to swarm around us looking for breakthroughs. Some of us had more syllables, others had fewer, but no matter what, we all learned how to get the gift of tongues that service.

From then on, that was the language I used to "pray in the Spirit." It was the language used to confuse the devil in prayer. It was the language that meant you had received the Holy Spirit. Most of all, it was the language that meant you were accepted by your parents and the rest of the church.

The Anointing of God

Services at our church—Vancouver Christian Center—were an experience like no other. We would sing for hours, endlessly speak in tongues, hear stories from the healing crusades that increased our faith, and give money in two offerings. On special Sundays (which could be any given Sunday), the anointing of God would descend on our church and God's power would cause people to fall over. As my dad prayed or anointed people with olive oil, they crumpled to the ground. We never referred to this event as being slain in the Spirit, though that is one way it's described. Instead, we joyously referred to it as "falling under the power."

People came from far and wide to take part in our church services. Even though by the midnineties our church had at most only a few hundred regular attenders, we always had visitors. Guest speakers were brought in to spice things up, and that meant our church was on the cutting edge of whatever new revelation they had. One guest speaker in particular ushered our church into the "holy water season." I remember his teaching: God was anointing water as a point of contact, and if people would drink the water or make contact with the water, they could get healed. He preached every night for a week, and I had never seen so many bottles of water in my short life. There were small ones, tall ones, five gallon ones, and every other form of bottled H_2O. People left services soaked in both water and the anointing of God. Bottles were taken to hospitals and deathbeds and kept in homes for the next time healing was needed. Healing in a bottle! I remember thinking, *Peter healed people with his shadow in the Bible; now we can do it with bottled water. God is so full of surprises.*

No matter the guest speakers who came through town, one

event was front and center at Vancouver Christian Center every single month: the Sunday night healing service. This wasn't your morning church crowd. During the 10:00 a.m. service, the church was half empty. At the 6:00 p.m. healing service on the first Sunday night of the month, however, the church was packed. These weren't people from our church. They were the desperate churchgoers from around the city who couldn't get healing at their Baptist, Presbyterian, or Lutheran churches, and so they came to us.

The structure of the healing services was identical to my uncle Benny's service at a crusade. My father made a grand entrance when the music hit its highest peak during worship, then he sang for a moment and prayed. The audience raised their hands a little higher and sang their songs a little louder. Expectancy filled the room. After nearly two solid hours of music and teaching, the transition began. "Hallelu-u-u-u-u-ah. Hallelu-u-u-u-u-ah," the band and my father sang in unison. Everybody knew what time it was. Nobody moved. My spine stiffened, and each time I felt my heart race. "Lift up your hands and pray in the Holy Spirit," my father commanded.

"*Shekundalabakasho. Shekundalabakasho*," I mumbled just loud enough to obey my dad but quiet enough not to be embarrassed. Even though everybody spoke in tongues, something always felt a bit off to me. We sounded silly, and my friends who visited our church always thought it was the weirdest thing. *Why don't they do it too?* I wondered.

As the murmuring of tongues in the room reached a roar, the singing erupted again and my dad commanded, "If you're sick in body, I want you to place your hand on the part of your body that is sick." Then he paused. "Loose! Loose! Loose!" he shouted with piercing authority. "You devil of infirmity! I command you to loose that body in Jesus' name!" Some people screamed, others fell, and many of us stood with eyes closed and hands raised, praying that God would heal people.

"Line up beside me if you have been healed and want God to touch you," the next set of instructions went. Ushers quickly scurried to the side of the stage, because the best part of the service was about to happen. Some three hours in, and we'd get to see who God healed!

I never saw people get healed real-time, but the testimonies were all the proof I needed. Sometimes people limped across the platform, but my dad always clarified, "When legs have been stuck in a wheelchair for many years, it takes some time for the muscles to loosen up and gain their strength." Every healing testimony was applauded, and a light touch from the healing hand sent people falling to be caught by catchers, who laid them gently down. Then, just like that, they were picked up, ushered off the stage, and sent onward to live healthily and happily ever after.

As the service wound down, an extra offering was often taken. With so many blessings and healings from God, it was obvious what we should do in return. It was time to give our best offering and seal the favor God had showered on us that night.

I always had a good night's sleep after the healing services in the early years. Sometimes they lasted until 11:00 p.m., but it didn't take long for me to fall asleep in the car. *Wow*, I would think. *Look at all God did tonight. I wish more people would open themselves up to experience this.*

Preacher's Kid

In many ways, I was the typical preacher's kid. Our family was under the constant microscope of both the church and the community, my siblings and I were always one wrong move away from a good spanking, and life revolved around church—pretty typical stuff for the families of pastors. On the other hand, my father had become a rather well-known Canadian televangelist-pastor and duplicated the ministry model my uncle leveraged to gain notoriety. While most pastors and their families live in a glass house, our life was a fortified utopian bubble. We were the center of our world with little friction from anyone inside it. Security personnel kept hecklers and threats at bay. Gated homes kept curious eyes from invading our privacy, and anybody who dared challenge our authority was threatened with divine judgment and excommunicated from the church.

My father would often tell us we were the most special family in the Christian world today and we should be proud that our uncle was the most anointed man of God of our day and age. It was clear that God had anointed us in a special way and provided us with special opportunities not everyone had. We were anointed with power, and we were to use that power to heal people and reveal the mysteries of God to them. Of course, having all of that power meant that we would (and should) benefit too. After all, we were the spiritual elite. We had direct access to God, and he spoke to us in ways few experienced. Why wouldn't we receive blessings for such selfless service as God's chosen vessels?

By an early age, as a part of the Hinn family, I viewed Jesus Christ as our magic genie—rub him right, and he'll give you whatever your heart desires. I quoted verses from the Bible like Psalm 37:4, which says, "Delight yourself in the LORD; And He will give you the desires of your heart," and John 14:14, where Jesus says, "If you ask Me anything in My name, I will do it." The meaning of these Scriptures was so obvious to me: believe in

Jesus Christ, ask for things by saying, "In Jesus' name," and you'll have whatever you want. Seriously—that simple. Not difficult to understand. Besides, it sure seemed to be working for us!

We were virtually untouchable when it came to sickness and disease. During flu season when people said, "The flu is going around," we would declare, "Yes, it is, and it's going *around* me, in Jesus' name!" (waving our hand around our body to signify that sickness was not stopping at our door). Death was never talked about in our house, disease was for people who had little faith and needed our help, and debt was a four-letter word we were always trying to get out of by taking bigger offerings. It was life in the fast lane of the prosperity gospel.

Birthdays for any kid are a big deal, but I counted down to birthdays with a unique thrill because I knew what was coming. Most teenage pastors' kids in the nineties probably got a birthday cake and maybe some knockoff Jordans. But for me, birthdays meant the nicest Italian restaurant in town and more than a thousand dollars in birthday money from church people alone. Everybody in the church gave me money. Add in checks from uncles, Grandpa, and Grandma, and I was loaded. Blessings and money weren't just for my parents; I was right in line to receive them as well.

Trouble in Paradise

Maybe it was the Benz dropping me off on the curb of the school we attended. Maybe it was the fancy clothes. Maybe it was the fact that their parents thought my dad and uncle were false teachers. Or maybe, instead of being anointed, I was really just an annoying classmate (more than likely). Whatever it was, kids at school were not nearly as enamored with me as the people from our church.

"Your uncle is a false teacher!" an older boy shouted one day as he slammed a glass door in my face and peered at me through it. I tried to open it up but to no avail. He was in fifth grade. I was in third. "Your uncle is Benny Hinn! He's the crazy guy on TV who knocks people over and steals all their money! Guess what? Your dad is a false teacher too and just as crazy as your stupid uncle!"

His words stung. What kid wouldn't be devastated to hear that said about their beloved father and uncle? I could feel my anger rising, but my physical strength fell far short of my strong emotions. I wrenched on the door once more and decided it was time to use words to do what my body couldn't. "Well, at least we have the power of God. You go to a dead church!" I roared back through the door. After that, I may or may not have cursed him with cancer and added a few other choice words.

It was survive or be eaten at the school, and I was often eaten. I acted out my frustration by being disrespectful and destructive during class, so I was often kicked out of class for misbehaving. If I couldn't control how others viewed me, then I couldn't care less what else happened.

Eventually, my sister and I convinced my parents to send us to Regent Christian Academy. It was a Foursquare denominational school where they raised their hands, spoke in tongues, and shared much of our brand of theology. We were finally going to be in the company of civilized church kids who understood our elite position in Christian society. No Baptists or other "dead" church denominations would cause me grief any longer.

Sixth grade began and things were going well at Regent. This meant there was no longer anyone to blame for my behavior but me. It wasn't long before my preteen arrogance merged with my theological beliefs to create a self-centered, entitled, and adventurous middle school monster. I was winning over my peers left and right and in turn defying teachers who dared to try to control me. What was supposed to be a more suitable environment for our belief system only served to flip the paradigm. At Richmond Christian School, we were bullied for our beliefs. Now, we used our beliefs to bully others—particularly, teachers. Since at Regent we were among fellow charismatic believers, teachers held some level of authority in our eyes, but we considered ourselves far more anointed than they were because we were elitists. Sure, they were the teachers at school, but if they came to our church, we could show them a thing or two about real knowledge and power. Armed with that attitude, I became a charismatic vigilante.

In eighth grade, I won a landslide victory to become class president, using my popularity with classmates to defeat my fellow candidate. My anointed status was outweighed only by my spiritual arrogance—who did this other kid think he was? I was a Hinn!

By February of that school year, I was leading a rebel group of students in full mutiny. In just five months of school, we had vandalized school property, broken into a neighboring Bible college basement to establish our headquarters, and been kicked out of class more times than I can recollect for mocking and disrespecting teachers.

Then came the final straw. I was sitting in chapel one afternoon with my best friend, Matt. We had caught a small snake and put it in a Skittles wrapper. Matt had the snake inside his shirt pocket. Chapel worship was in full swing. Girls sat in chairs from the back to the halfway point in the room, while boys sat on the floor from the halfway point in the room to the front. Matt and I were in the back row of the boys' section—only feet away from the girls. I kept trying to flick the snake-filled wrapper out of his pocket, and he kept swatting my hand away. Finally, I succeeded. All I remember is the clanking sound of metal chairs and girls screaming at the top of their lungs. Then, the familiar smell of the principal's office.

Expelled by late February, I was given passing grades, was sent various assignments to be done at home, and enjoyed a summer vacation from March to September. During this break from school, I played hockey on my sport court, swam in our heated pool, and went on ministry trips with my father to Singapore and Jakarta.

Ready for a new school with far fewer rules and no uniforms, we enrolled in what is still considered one of the best Christian high schools in British Columbia. At the time, it was called Fraser Valley Christian High. It was Christian Reformed, a denomination based in the Calvinist theological tradition and founded by hardworking, frugal Dutch immigrants—a church not exactly known for its sympathies toward faith-healing prosperity preachers. I had hoped for a fresh start, but two weeks into the fall semester, word had gotten around about my last name. *Oh, no*, I thought, *not again*.

The student who had taken particular notice was a boy we'll call "Aaron," but at six foot three, he was no boy. After enduring his insults and mockery about my Hinn family heritage, I was not about to let anyone degrade my anointed uncle or my heroic father ever again. In the library, I did something I regret to this day.

We were in the midst of Bible class when Mr. Terpstra, our

teacher, gave us instructions to do group assignments in the library. As we talked among ourselves, Aaron quipped, "It must suck to be the nephew of Benny Hinn and the son of Henry Hinn." Some other boys sneered along with him.

I didn't know what to say. I was a small, prepubescent late bloomer who barely had the strength to bench-press the bar without a weight on it. But this was the big leagues now. It was time to make a statement.

As we walked to the library, I imagined all the things I could do to quiet Aaron's bullying. Then I noticed an area where students left backpacks and other items not allowed in the library. There it was. A skateboard.

The most evil thought came to mind.

I made a mental note to come back and get it once we were all settled in our groups. Aaron was over in the corner with some of the boys when the moment came. I walked out of the library, picked up the skateboard, and walked right back through the library to where he was sitting. Skateboard in hand, I swung at his head with all I had. There were cries of astonishment and shouts of, "He's bleeding!" as Aaron slumped to the table. I found Mr. Terpstra and handed him the skateboard. In shock, he ran past me, and I walked out of the library unhindered, eventually finding a stump outside the school to sit on.

Within ten minutes, I heard the sirens. Mr. Terpstra came out of the school, walked over to me, and said, "There you are. I was looking for you. Are you okay?"

Am I okay? Is he serious? I just hit the biggest kid in class in the head with a skateboard. Am I okay?

When I didn't answer, he said, "We should probably head to the office, eh?"

I nodded and followed him back into the school.

Everything else that day was a blur. I felt terrible for what I had done but knew I had to defend my family's honor and not let people speak against my anointed uncle and father. Those men were my heroes. Who was anyone to spread lies about them and call them horrible things?

The principal should have expelled me. Actually, I should have been arrested. Instead, I was given three weeks' suspension and told that after Aaron got out of the hospital, he would be suspended for one week for bullying me. Who would have thought? A Christian Reformed school showing me grace when I deserved wrath.

The suspension allowed time for me to cool off, meet with the discipline committee, and review the plan for restoring me to school. At the meeting, I had to face Aaron and his parents. Aaron's father was certainly not amused—who could blame him? But before the meeting began, Aaron's mother walked right up to me and said, "You just need a hug." And she hugged me!

What in the world is wrong with these people? I thought. At the time, I believed I had a special anointing they most certainly didn't have. Looking back, I can see they were the ones who possessed something I didn't have. Grace.

3

The Laws of Prosperity

Those that fail to learn from history are
doomed to repeat it.

—WINSTON CHURCHILL

"Tonight is a special night. Jesus is here, and he always keeps his
promises. I want you to lift up your hands and ask the Lord Jesus
for anything you want—he will give it to you! He has come to
give us life and life more abundantly!"

The sound of my uncle Benny's voice echoed through the
stadium as he finished his healing crusade message. The crowd
of twenty thousand rumbled as people flooded heaven with
their petitions. Some asked Jesus to give them healing, houses,
and promotions at work. Others asked Jesus for the salvation of
a loved one. Others just wanted cold hard cash. I couldn't blame

them—that was one of God's biggest ways of showing his favor to people. My uncle had used the Bible to clearly explain that God promises to give loads of money to people who give loads of money to him. Who could argue with that?

At age fifteen, my adrenaline fired, my heart raced, and my imagination ran wild with big dreams. This was my moment! It was time to tap into the special anointing that Uncle Benny was channeling. With total assurance in the lesson we'd been taught, I closed my eyes and with every ounce of sincerity my heart could muster, I pleaded, "Dear Jesus, please let me play Major League Baseball and be wealthy so my family will never have any lack. And please keep me from ever being sick."

What a special opportunity, I thought. Now, all I had to do was trust in God and wait for my dreams to come true.

No Money? No Miracle!

In 1999, Benny Hinn was the most famous and controversial prosperity preacher and faith healer in the world. But to me, he was my anointed uncle whom God was using to show us how to live a life of blessing and abundance. It was the way God intended everyone to live—we were living proof!

In one sermon I heard growing up, my uncle taught us that if we wanted God to do something for us, we needed to do something for him. This applied to everything—especially miracles. Whenever possible, Benny would preach to the masses that if they wanted a miracle for their sickness and disease, they needed to give money to God. No money? No miracle! Giving to God was the secret to unlocking your dreams. It was the secret to job promotions. It was access to our divine bank account. My uncle often told the story of how he got out of debt using this system of belief. His father-in-law had told him that in order to be debt free, he needed to pay God. Benny explained that once he started emptying his bank account and giving money away to ministry, money started showing up from everywhere!

This principle on giving was a serious one in our family. We believed we could be guilty of robbing God if we weren't giving him enough, so there were times that retroactive payments were necessary. I remember thinking, *For all the time I have spent living for my own pleasures, I will need to devote nearly two years to God if I am to have my prayers answered and fulfilled.*

One of Uncle Benny's heroes who taught him about this system of believing, giving, and receiving was Oral Roberts. It seemed he could open the windows of heaven and cause them to rain down blessings on his own life. It was a simple money-in, money-out transaction, with God as the banker. Oral Roberts wanted to help more people understand it and take the risk to put it into practice. He taught that this way of thinking was used by Jesus and the apostles. For Roberts, it was faith that forced God to do what we wanted him to do. Believing enough, thinking positively enough, and giving enough could control the Creator! Roberts had used his teachings on money and faith to rise out of obscurity and into stardom, then helped others do the same.[1] Now, so was my uncle.

Over decades, Roberts coached my uncle Benny and they

---

1 On using money and faith to get what you want, Roberts says, "The seed of giving is the seed of faith! And the seed has to be planted before we can speak to our mountain of need to be removed!" (Oral Roberts, *A Daily Guide to Miracles* [Tulsa: Pinoak Publications, 1975], 63). This teaching argues that the key to forcing God's blessings to rain down on one's life is to give money.

became close friends. Uncle Benny and Oral would shoot television programs together, share ideas, and promote each other within their respective ministries. This sort of "stage sharing" was how ministries exploded onto new frontiers. Oral's audience became Uncle Benny's, and vice versa.

Cancer in the Family

For a long time, things went well for the Hinn family. We were happy, healthy, and rich. But inevitably, real life intruded for my mom's side of the family. That's when we went into damage control mode.

When I was in fourth grade, my uncle George was diagnosed with cancer. He was not an actual uncle but rather my mom's cousin's husband. He had been pastoring at our church after my dad hired him, and I thought the world of him. He had the gentlest smile, always called me Tiger, and gave me those affectionate headlock hugs that uncles give. We were saddened by his diagnosis.

At the time, his son Adam was my best friend at both church and school. Adam was having a tough time with his dad's battle with cancer, and I remember vividly when our teacher, Mrs. Friesen, one day asked him how he was doing. Adam shrugged off her question with a quick, "Fine."

After she walked away, I looked at him. "You don't like talking about it, do you?" I asked.

He shook his head no. With five kids in the family, my uncle George and my auntie Debbie were facing a monumental challenge.

The situation worsened. After a skin graft, the best efforts of doctors, and our prayers for healing, Uncle George experienced a stroke, along with setbacks to his health that eventually led to his passing away. It was devastating. Sunday after Sunday, we heard from the pulpit, "God has guaranteed healing! Just have faith and God will do whatever you ask him to do." So many people had been brought up on stage and declared healed. So many people, but not Uncle George? Only one explanation could satisfy the confusing question that became the elephant in every room we occupied: *How in the world did he not get healed?*

Before I knew it, my auntie Debbie had distanced herself and my five second cousins from us and the church. Intense drama unfolded as other people left both before and after that time, including my mom's brothers. It was a mass exodus of people we were close to. *Why, God?* I wondered. *Was it because of Uncle George? Other reasons?* It hurt so bad to see Uncle George die, but why did all these people I loved have to leave the church as well? We were supposed to be family. And our family was supposed to be different—blessed and anointed.

Soon we were given an explanation for his death. We rationalized that Uncle George (and his family) must have done one or more of the "big four," which caused him to lose whatever declared healing he was guaranteed. The big four, or a short list of reasons why God didn't heal people, went something like this:

- Making a negative confession: using negative words about your physical condition would hinder your healing.
- Hanging around negative people: allowing the negative words of others about your physical condition would hinder your healing.
- Not having enough faith: not believing or giving enough money to prove your trust that God would heal you.

- Touching the Lord's anointed: speaking against or
  opposing a man of God who is anointed.

Turns out, as the story went, that Uncle George and the people
around him did all four of these. Most of all, we were told that
Uncle George had started to hang around with people who spoke
negatively about my father and our church. There was a zero-
tolerance policy in our belief system for this sort of thing.

The "touching the Lord's anointed" teaching came from a
biblical principle observed in the Old Testament. In 1 Samuel
24:6, King David had just held back from an opportunity to kill
his enemy and attacker, King Saul. He sneaked up on him and cut
a small piece of King Saul's robe off and later showed it to him
as a sign that he meant him no harm and could have killed him
but didn't. The principle that guided David was that King Saul
was still an anointed king of Israel and it was not David's place to
kill him or "touch" him. On this Old Testament principle of not
killing kings, our church took touching the Lord's anointed very
seriously.

The story I was eventually told is that Uncle George started
playing softball on Sundays to try to stay active during his battle
with cancer, which was a serious no-no in our legalistic church.
When my father confronted him about this, Uncle George did not
follow orders and perhaps had a few other opinions as well. Since
Uncle George had begun to hang around with negative people
who weren't mesmerized by my father, they had corrupted his
life and removed him from God's favor. While playing softball
one day and rounding third base, Uncle George had a stroke and
collapsed, doctors could do nothing for him, and he eventually
died because he let negative people into his hospital room and

into his life. That was the simple explanation. Whether or not this was true, it was the simple explanation.

Many people left the church over the following years, and if they died anytime after leaving the church, they also joined the illustration file of those who had touched the Lord's anointed. Many others, however, chose to stay, believing that God's favor and protection were contingent on their staying under my father's leadership. Throughout the nineties, the same storyline was revealed in my uncle Benny's ministry as well. Some of his ex-employees were dying, and others, like my aunt Karen, who had voiced her displeasure with his ministry antics and handling of money, were suddenly struck with illness. All of this served as proof that we were anointed by God. Mess with us, and you'll be under a divine death sentence.

Despite the exodus of church members and dwindling Sunday attendance, my family knew no lack. Somehow money kept pouring in and blessings kept raining down.

Putting Seed-Faith into Practice

By the time I reached high school graduation, I had dreams of my own, and I was determined to see those dreams become a reality. But first, I needed to put into practice one of our theological beliefs: that of sowing my seeds of faith. I believed that if I sacrificed something now for the kingdom of God, I would reap untold benefits later on.

Kenneth Copeland, a self-proclaimed billionaire prosperity preacher and one of my childhood heroes, said, "There are certain laws governing prosperity revealed in God's Word. Faith causes them to function. They will work when they are put to work, and they will stop working when the force of faith is stopped."[2] Gloria Copeland, his wife, taught that God's will is always prosperity and that not only does Jesus give a hundredfold return to sacrificial followers on earth (Mark 10:29–30), but we can tap into the hundredfold return on earth. The hundredfold return works like this: "You give $1.00 for the gospel's sake and the full hundredfold return would be $100. Ten dollars would be $1,000. A hundredfold return on $1,000 would be $100,000 . . . Mark 10:30 is a very good deal."[3] With my eyes set on achieving my dream of living the abundant life God intended for me to live, I knew I had to put my faith into action to make things happen. The Copelands' teaching on the hundredfold return for giving would guide my way.

According to Kenneth, the whole kingdom of God operates according to the principles of planting, seedtime, and harvest. The hundredfold return is God's principle of return on your giving. What are you planting in the kingdom of God? Expect a hundredfold return on whatever you give, whether it be words, faith, money, or any other seed you plant. So how much is a hundredfold exactly? We often think of it as a hundred times the amount of seed sown, but it can be much greater than that. The hundredfold return is simply the greatest possible return on any seed sown.[4]

I had heard about and witnessed many stories that seemed

2   Kenneth Copeland, The Laws of Prosperity (Fort Worth: Kenneth Copeland Publications, 1974), 15.

3   Gloria Copeland, God's Will Is Prosperity (Fort Worth: Kenneth Copeland Publications, 1978), 71.

4   "How Much Is a Hundredfold Return?" Kenneth Copeland Ministries, http://www.kcm. org/read/questions/how-much-hundredfold-return.

to corroborate the Copelands' teaching. I'll never forget how, as a young boy, I went with my parents to pay a pastoral call on a widow named Marina. While I played, they talked for hours, and at the end of the meeting, she gave my parents one million dollars. Stories like this were common. As long as we were faithful to God and sowed seed into good ministry soil (or to anointed leaders), God would give us back a harvest that was far beyond what we gave.

At the time, I thought, *God will give me a hundred times or even more back if I give him something! The only reason people must live in poverty or mediocrity is because they lack the faith it takes to live in abundance.* I was the master of my own destiny—the captain of my soul! It was time to tap into the hundredfold blessing by living out my faith and sowing my time as a seed. I wasn't going to be riding on the coattails of my parents' faith. This would be striking out on my own to give and receive.

My uncle had been asking me to work with him for a couple of years, but I kept telling him I was going to college to play baseball. But now, I had learned what it means to go all-in for God. Maybe it was time to really put God first and sow some seed-faith into the soil. Surely God would unleash his blessings upon my dreams if I gave up an entire year of college baseball to serve Uncle Benny.

Luke 6:38 is a prooftext I used for this transaction. Prooftext is the term for taking a passage from the Bible out of its context in order to prove your point. It's a lot like interpreting a document the way you want to and not the way the author intended. This particular prooftext says, "Give, and it will be given to you. They will pour into your lap a good measure—pressed down, shaken together, and running over. For by your standard of measure, it will be measured to you in return." In my mind, serving Uncle Benny was my first step if I wanted to achieve my dream of becoming a Major League Baseball player.

Soon, I was excited to hear affirmations of my decision. To sow my seed of faith into my uncle's ministry over other ministry options was a wise one because of the fertile soil it provided. "He is the greatest man of God in the world," one family member declared. "Nobody is as anointed as he is. God is going to bless your life in a powerful way for serving your uncle Benny," another family member told me. I had taken the leap of faith that would seal my future.

In that moment, with my dreams for a career in baseball on hold, it felt like I was giving up my life for Jesus just like the disciples did.

4

Living the Abundant Life

God wants you to succeed; he created you
to live abundantly.

—JOEL OSTEEN

"I hate you! I hate you! I hate you!"

My dad, driving his newly acquired Ferrari F430, had just pulled into Uncle Benny's driveway. Spotting him from the front steps of his California beachfront property, Benny shouted a playful greeting: "I hate you!"

This visit to Uncle Benny was marked by a little brotherly competition. The prosperity gospel pays amazingly well, and so do shady business deals that go on in the background, and we had the toys to prove it. This particular Ferrari came as a result of a business deal with my father's and uncle's cousin Harold Hinn. In the prosperity gospel world, it is perfectly normal to mix ministry with business and use ministry money to fund business ventures. Harold was a known scam artist who had cheated some other family members out of money and we'd been warned to be wary of him, but my father had already been made an offer he couldn't refuse. This deal eventually went terribly wrong and resulted in Harold's laundering and losing more than $1.3 million dollars. Two banks, a casino, and a whole lot of our church members' money were involved. One lawsuit later and we almost lost everything. Harold ended up getting arrested for fraud.

But for now, Harold had sent the Ferrari as part of the deal, and it was ours to enjoy! I sat in the passenger seat laughing as Uncle Benny came out to see it. Sometimes we cheered on the blessings of others; sometimes they cheered on ours. On this particular day, we "won." Our Ferrari beat out his Bentley. It was all God's blessings on our lives anyway, so we were just having a little family fun.

This was our normal.

The Job Description

Growing up in the prosperity gospel is one thing. Working on the inside of it is another. As a young boy, I just went along for the ride. But as a paid adult, I had duties within the ministry and took ownership of understanding how things worked. I had to do what I could to ensure that the Hinn family was cared for.

My job was to be one of my uncle's personal assistants when we traveled and to be a catcher during the healing services. I also served in this capacity with my father when we traveled for ministry events.

As a personal assistant, I carried cash—a lot of cash. Usually it was housed in a fanny pack (preferably Louis Vuitton) and contained tip money for hotel managers, restaurant servers, and chauffeurs and for petty cash spending needs. Additional duties included carrying luggage and personal bags, checking in and out of hotels, handing magazines to the boss and putting on his favorite DVDs on our flights, handing our group's passports to customs agents who boarded our private plane, paying the restaurant check, and arranging the setup of cabanas, chairs, and towels at hotel pools.

As a catcher, I stood on the stage with my father or uncle, and when people "fell under their power" (or what many Christians call being slain in the Spirit), I caught them. The act of falling is triggered when the faith healer touches a person and shouts a phrase such as, "Fire!" or, "Heal!" Catchers need to be ready at all times. There are moments when catchers need to catch multiple people, keep up with a feverish pace of falling people, or are knocked over themselves by the faith healer. Quick reflexes are imperative. All in a day's work.

The Benefits Plan

When we're talking prosperity gospel benefits, I don't mean medical coverage. I mean *material* coverage. In less than just two years of working within the movement (not including growing up in it), I enjoyed more luxury than I ever could have imagined. It felt like I was hanging out with King Solomon. There are wealthy people who have lots of money but don't live lavishly; then there are wealthy people who have lots of money and know how to turn lavish novelty into normalcy. We were the latter.

Here's a sample of the travel arrangements, hotels, and shopping spree destinations I experienced during that almost two-year period:

- Air travel on a Gulfstream IV (average cost of ownership: $36,000,000)
- Royal Suite at the Burj Al Arab in Dubai, United Arab Emirates ($25,000 per night)
- Villa d'Este, Lake Como, Italy (near where George Clooney owns a lake house)
- The Vatican, Vatican City, Rome
- The Grand Resort Lagonissi, Greece (villas set on the Aegean Sea)
- The Lanesborough Hotel (London)
- The Mandarin Oriental, Mumbai, India
- The Ritz-Carlton, Paris
- The Ritz-Carlton, Laguna Niguel, California
- Shopping spree at Harrods in London
- Shopping spree up and down Rodeo Drive, Beverly Hills, California
- Hotel suites at the Hotel de Paris, Monte-Carlo, Monaco
- Gambling at the Casino de Monte-Carlo, Monaco
- Shopping spree in Monte-Carlo, Monaco
- Tours of Israel
- Presidential suite at the Grand Wailea, Maui, Hawaii
- Private beach house, Kona, Hawaii
- Vehicle chauffeurs in Bentley, Rolls-Royce, Mercedes-Benz, Range Rover, Maserati
- Apparel by Versace, Salvatore Ferragamo, Gucci, Bijan
- Accessories by Louis Vuitton, Prada, Breitling, Chanel, Hermes, D&G

Wealthy people who enjoy the finer things in life look at this list and shrug. Perhaps even people with modest levels of income say, "Big deal, so you enjoyed nice stuff." Both are right to view it with indifference—until we remind ourselves that this was paid for by donations from desperate people who believed that giving a prosperity preacher their money would result in their living this lifestyle too. Somewhat more heartbreaking is that some of these donors were just hoping to see a fifty-cent increase above their minimum wage as a blessing from God for sowing their seed. The hardest working people were the poor barely making it but giving everything to us.

I remember when I first realized that our lifestyle was fueled by taking advantage of others and supported by volunteers and employees who didn't live anything like us. I was in my late teens on a trip to visit my uncle in California. He had a married couple, "Ron" and "Sarah," who served as his personal butler and maid for many years. They had been with him in Florida and had been moved to California by the ministry to serve him there as well.

On this visit, Ron picked me up from the airport, and for some reason I started to talk to him about his life. Come to find out, they commuted one hour each way every day to work at my uncle's house in Orange County. They had to live an hour away because Orange County is one of the most expensive places to live in the US. They lived very modestly while working in my uncle's $8.2 million-dollar ocean-view mansion, driving a beat-up mini-van and working themselves to the bone to care for their kids and make ends meet.

That day, the contrast hit me like a ton of bricks. Here they were working as full-time servants for my uncle and they could barely afford to live. Ron cooked the meals, packed for my uncle, got his car washed and detailed for him, dusted his car with a feather duster before it left the garage each day, did the grocery shopping for the family, took out the trash, walked the dog, and everything in between. Sarah made every bed, cleaned every bathroom, washed every floor, ironed every shirt, and windexed every window. Yet I had barely noticed them in all the years I'd known them.

Of course a lot of wealthy people employ housekeepers and butlers. But shouldn't a pastor be different in how he cares for his employees? *Maybe this is why my uncle's ministry has so much turnover,* I thought.

Something didn't seem right. But I was just a teenager, so I pushed the doubts and misgivings out of my mind.

Fool's Gold

I'll never forget the trip to Dubai.

Our flight landed at the airport in the early afternoon. The heat of the day would soon be upon us, and I couldn't wait to go for a swim. As our Gulfstream IV came to a stop, the door opened and we remained seated. Up the stairs came customs agents who did passport checks right there on the plane. While the rest of the world waits in two-hour customs lines, private plane travelers enjoy the VIP treatment. No baggage claim sweat, no crowds, no hassle. I was glad to see the process going so quickly because I couldn't wait to get to the hotel.

Having seen the Burj Al Arab on the Travel Channel, I figured this was bound to be as close as a human being could get to experiencing Solomon's Temple. We were booked in the royal suite—accommodations fit for only the filthy rich. Even the hotel pens were said to have brushed gold on them.

As we approached the pickup area, I scanned the curb for our motorcade. Sure enough, there it was. Clutching my uncle Benny's Louis Vuitton suitcase, I approached three white luxury cars and got into one as soon as he was safely in the lead vehicle. The hotel offered multiple choices for pickup, including Rolls-Royces, a helicopter, and BMWs, but no matter what, luxury was the name of the game.

From the moment the cars left the airport, we began excitedly discussing the hotel. "Apparently there is gold everywhere!" said one of our security personnel.

"Like real gold? How much could they possibly have?" I asked.

Our driver, who was a local, declared that we were about to witness the greatest hotel on earth. In just a short time, we crossed a bridge through a guarded entrance and onto the hotel's man-made island to the striking sail-shaped building. We discovered that the hotel did indeed have real gold—approximately twenty-two thousand feet of it. Twenty-four-carat gold leaf covered the interior of the hotel, including the TV screens. As if that wasn't enough, we had our choice of seventeen types of pillows, an 8,400-square-foot royal suite (not including the three other suites we had for security and ministry leaders), and a private butler. The donations of our faithful partners footed a bill of approximately forty thousand dollars for the overnight trip. In our eyes, our hotel stay was well deserved. Such restful layovers were an essential part of the prosperity gospel travel plan.

A proof text that we went back to time and again says, "'YOU SHALL NOT MUZZLE THE OX WHILE HE IS THRESHING,' and 'The laborer is worthy of his wages'" (1 Tim. 5:18). The apostle Paul is explaining that pastors should be paid in such a way that enables them to minister. In our eyes, we were laboring for the cause of Christ by putting in all that hard work of travel and ministry. Grueling services lasted nearly four hours, hundreds needed to be caught after being slain in the Spirit, and we were praying for the sick. Our schedule demanded continuous travel because of the great needs of hurting people. We had to rest well and be paid well to be ready to minister to them effectively.

Prosperity Gospel Vandals

While I certainly behaved like a minister during the healing services, my hotel and nightlife behavior was a different story. On a trip to Paris, I roomed with my cousin at the Ritz-Carlton. Being a classy place, the Ritz had a dress code. You couldn't even wear jeans! Well, my cousin and I let them know just how much we respected the Ritz dress code by trashing our room with a food fight. With our body clocks operating on Pacific Time, my cousin and I stayed up all night, ordered room service repeatedly, and launched food at each other until the early hours of the morning. We behaved like spoiled children, staining the wallpaper with fruit and having no regard for the expensive furniture that filled the lavish room. In the morning when we checked out of our hotel, barely a word was spoken about the incident, but one of the security personnel on our team gave us a stern talk. Apparently they had forked over five thousand euros to satisfy the hotel. My uncle never heard anything about it.

The hypocrisy and wild behavior weren't limited to the inside of our hotel rooms. On many trips we frequented bars and nightclubs, spending thousands of dollars and enjoying our own version of prosperity living. Just hours after working in a healing service and putting on a gospel show, we would be out on the town. With thousands in tip money at our disposal and our own security detail, we behaved like celebrities and racked up the tab. On top of that, we were paid well for single guys, so having enough money was never an issue. Of course, this behavior served as evidence of our phony Christianity, but we just felt like we were blowing off steam. Most of the time, the security team was just trying to keep us alive so my uncle wouldn't fire them. Looking back, I realize those men had to deal with a lot.

California, Here We Come

By 2003–2004 our lifestyle was really ramping up. My father and I kept a rigorous schedule, traveling both for his ministry and for Uncle Benny. We would be home for a few days here and there, then head back out on the crusade circuit. Money was pouring in. Flying around the world felt like a normal commute to work.

Around that same time, my older sister got married and moved to Florida. With just two kids left at home—my younger sister and me—my parents decided to make a long-desired move as well, to Orange County, California. We were going to keep the nearly ten-thousand-square-foot mansion in Canada (valued at just over three million), but by adding a two-million-dollar ocean-view home in California, we finally had the perfect life. Two homes, in two beautiful West Coast locations, serving the Lord and helping people. What could be better?

Life in California was incredible. The first car I owned after moving there was a Cadillac Escalade, but after a couple of years, I grew bored with it. It felt old and I dreamed of something bigger and better, so I upgraded to a brand new Hummer. At just twenty-one years old, I was riding in style. My Hummer (H2) was black, fully loaded, with twenty-two-inch rims, a chrome package front to back, televisions in every headrest, limo tint on all the windows, and a thousand-dollar monthly payment because, why not? We never put a lot of money down on anything because we could always make the high payment and wouldn't have to part with lump sums of cash. That was the way I was taught to handle my finances.

We ate at Orange County's top restaurants on a weekly basis. Sometimes we'd enjoy a night out with our family, and other times we'd meet up with Paul Crouch (founder of Trinity Broadcasting Network) at a favorite restaurant. The who's who of prosperity gospel preaching always stuck together.

But with each purchase and lifestyle addition, the demand for funding increased. Add in the rat race of keeping up with the prosperity gospel Joneses, and you've got all the motivation required to do whatever needs to be done to solicit cash from donors. Trips became more frequent, the travel a mixture of international and domestic. Messages on television from my uncle would always get more outlandish based on how much money the ministry needed to raise. Special guests like Mike Murdock or Steve Munsey would be brought in to really get the crowd going, because these men were considered expert fundraisers who'd made millions for ministries like ours. Much like a nonprofit company will hire a donor relations specialist who works to create a network of supporters for a good cause, the prosperity gospel uses its network of money men (and women) to increase offerings. Once the money was made, things would settle down again for a little while.

It's no wonder the prosperity gospel is such a hustle—the salaries we made were enormous. It wasn't uncommon for my father to make thirty-five thousand dollars on a single trip. We were paid lump sums per travel day, and per service. When you accumulate the travel days, the number of services, and the offering numbers, the payday is huge if you're on the inside. It was no sweat (just a lot of travel) to make close to half a million dollars a year.

For the top earners in the prosperity gospel, half a million dollars a year is tip money. In 2011 *Forbes* compiled a list of some of the world's richest preachers. Using only Nigeria in one of their reports, the top five preachers earned $150 million, $30–50 million, $10–15 million, $6–10 million, and $3–10 million.[1]

Another report in 2017 listed the richest pastors in the world, and prosperity gospel names topped the list. Names on the list included Kenneth Copeland ($760 million), T. D. Jakes ($150 million), Benny Hinn ($42 million), Joel Osteen ($40 million), Creflo Dollar ($27 million), and Joyce Meyer ($25 million).[2]

We're Just Like Jesus and Paul

It was during all of this prosperity gospel pleasure that I finally took a moment to relish it all. Life was moving fast and everything seemed to be falling in line with God's will for me. I was blessed.

Standing on a rock ledge just outside of Athens, I took it all in. There I was, staying at one of the most beautiful hotels in the world. The Grand Resort Lagonissi was set on a sea cove with nothing between me and the water but the rocks. I had my very

---

1 Mfonobong Nsehe, "The Five Richest Pastors in Nigeria," *Forbes*, June 7, 2011, https://www.forbes.com/sites/mfonobongnsehe/2011/06/07/the-five-richest-pastors-in-nigeria/#65e9fa886031.

2 "Top Fifteen Richest and Most Successful Pastors in the World," *ETInside*, July 9, 2018, http://www.etinside.com/?p=539.

own private two-thousand-square-foot villa, complete with private pool and massive yard. Sliding doors opened across the front of the entire suite, and every night I fell asleep to the sound of the ocean breeze. As I looked out over the water that day, I thought, I *have arrived*. This was it. My life was set. I was traveling the world taking the gospel to the ends of the earth just like Jesus said to do. I was part of a ministry that was healing the sick and hurting across the globe. I would be an anointed man of God just like my uncle and father. It had been prophesied over me since I was a young boy that I would carry on the family legacy of faith and propel the family name to greater heights. Now that my uncle and father had paved the way, all that was left for me to do was finish out my seed-faith commitment to Uncle Benny's ministry, play some baseball, graduate from college, and then jump right into ministry.

As I peered out from those rocks that day, I was staring at the Aegean Sea, the same body of water that the apostle Paul sailed on his missionary journeys.

There was just one problem: we weren't preaching the same gospel as Paul.

5

Unanswered Questions

The Lord told me it's flat none of your business.

—JIMMY SWAGGART

When I was growing up within the prosperity gospel, I enjoyed it. When I worked on the inside of the prosperity gospel, I profited from it. But when I saw what appeared to be shortcomings of the prosperity gospel, I questioned it. Answers were often elusive. For all the confidence I had in the life I was living, serious doubts stirred. Lavish hotels and big money made for great bandaids, but they couldn't stop the questions from eventually bleeding through.

A number of experiences during that time provoked questions that eventually put a crack in the foundation of my deepest beliefs.

Making Millions of Dollars

In the summer of 2003, the Los Angeles Times released a report that made some waves. Writing about the revenue of our ministry in the prior year, William Lobdell states,

> The hands of faith healer Benny Hinn—tools of a televangelist recognized around the world—are slim, almost feminine. The fingers are delicate, nails manicured and polished. A gold wedding band, so wide it covers the bottom of his left ring finger from knuckle to knuckle like a piece of copper pipe, bears the insignia of his church. The dove, symbolizing the Holy Spirit, sparkles with a cluster of diamonds.
>
> These small, soft hands could be one of two things: anointed by God to heal the sick, or props in a televangelist money-making scheme that preys on the vulnerable. Shades of gray aren't a part of the Benny Hinn story. Financially, at least, he's the world's most successful faith healer, having received $89 million in donations last year, according to officials with his ministry, World Healing Center Church. His followers pack stadiums here and abroad for his free events called "Miracle Crusades." He conducts about twenty-four of these each year, traveling in a leased Gulfstream jet. Attendance averages 50,000 to 60,000 people over two days, with a crusade in Kenya two years ago drawing 1.2 million worshippers, organizers say.[1]

Ouch! Who does this guy think he is? I scoffed. Sure, it looked

---

1 William Lobdell, "The Price of Healing," Los Angeles Times, July 27, 2003, http://articles .latimes.com/2003/jul/27/magazine/tm-benny30.

like we made a lot of money, but this reporter obviously didn't understand the principles of giving and receiving. Our ministries were blessed with millions because we were a blessing to others. I guess the way we solicited donations could be considered scandalous if someone like Lobdell twisted it into juicy newspaper gossip, but it could also be considered spiritual, couldn't it?

Around that time, an experience in Finland left serious doubts in my mind about the methods we used to get money out of followers.

An Anointed Exchange

We were on our way to Helsinki to do some ministry. Only around five thousand people were anticipated to attend the service, a slightly different vibe than the usual mass crusades. We arrived in Helsinki on a cold, foggy winter day. I love that kind of weather, and the historic architecture interwoven with brick sidewalks and the drapery of leafless oak trees only enhanced the beautiful landscape.

As the service filled to capacity on the final night of the trip, my father, who was leading the service that night, told the crowd to put their best offering in the envelopes. The ushers started handing out envelopes row by row. It was a moment of money manipulation that seared my conscience.

"Get me the oil," he told one of our team members. The man reached for the bottle of olive oil under his seat.

In many Pentecostal and charismatic religious services, olive oil is believed to be a symbolic "point of contact" for anointing. A point of contact is an item used for transferring divine power to people. Going far beyond that, prosperity-gospel and faith-healing leaders use olive oil to coerce people into giving money. Since olive oil was believed to be a special substance for getting God's anointing, a prosperity preacher would look out into the crowd and make an offer for an anointed exchange. It was God's anointing being applied to your life for healing, money, conception of children, job promotions, and more in exchange for a monetary offering that would be prayed over and anointed with the oil. It was a divine transaction that appealed to the deepest human needs. It tugged on the most sensitive heartstrings. A typical solicitation from the platform might sound something like this:

Some of you are believing God for the salvation of your lost children. Some of you have sick babies and loved ones who are dying. Some of you are unable to conceive children and have been believing God for years. Others of you need jobs, or are in debt, or have been believing God for a financial breakthrough. This is your moment! There is a special anointing here tonight for breakthroughs. I want you to sow a seed of faith into God's kingdom, and he will bless you with whatever you are asking him for. I'm going to anoint every single offering envelope, but only if you put your best seed inside of it. The ushers are passing around the envelopes. Sow your seed, then come down the aisles to the platform. I'm going to lay hands on you and anoint your offering as you place it in the buckets here on stage.

Of all the methods we used for raising money, I had never before noticed just how slimy this one seemed (no pun intended). As much as I liked when revenue was high, some methods went a bit too far, even for us.

I cringed. It was as though suddenly I had a conscience. Is he going to do what I think he is going to do? Yep.

"Put your offering in the envelopes and come forward. I am going to anoint your envelope with oil and pray over you as you give it," my father instructed. "God is going to bless you for giving sacrificially tonight!"

The conviction of the Holy Spirit was so intense. My stomach was in knots. I could have sunk into my seat and happily died right there just to avoid the scene. After noticing a few people scowling uncomfortably, I kept my head down the entire time. These people seemed somewhat conservative. They were quite bothered by what was happening but kept on bringing offering envelopes to be anointed with oil. They must have come for fear of being the only ones not to come.

On the way back to the hotel, I angrily questioned my father but was quickly silenced.

"There's nothing wrong with imparting the anointing on people's lives for their obedience and giving their money for it, Costi," he scolded. "God will bless them for it, and we are blessed for offering it to them."

Our team had a meeting in our hotel room to count the offering. We divided the spoils among ourselves. Payment for the anointed impartation.

Something inside didn't feel right. We were never invited back.

A Crowd of Millions

Helsinki, with its puny crowd of five thousand, was a one-off. If there was a ranking system for the top attendance drawn by any faith healer in a lifetime, Benny Hinn's name has to be somewhere near the top. It's not uncommon for him to draw crowds in the hundreds of thousands in countries like Brazil, Nigeria, or Kenya. He's even had crowds that number in the millions at a single healing crusade. Our trip to Mumbai in 2004 was the first time in our ministry's history that we eclipsed seven figures for an event. The sights, sounds, and smells of that trip fill my memory to this day.

"Close the door! Close the door!" shouted my uncle from the comfort of our aircraft.

I hadn't been to India before, so I wasn't sure what all the fuss was about.

"I don't want to deal with the smell until I absolutely have to," he explained to the flight attendant who had begun to open the aircraft door. Customs wasn't coming our way yet, so Uncle Benny didn't want the door opened. Apparently India had an aroma that my uncle didn't care for.

Later as we drove through the streets of Mumbai, I marveled at the wild traffic. Cars zipped in and out of lanes—which didn't really exist—so fast and chaotically that one could only hope to make it through unscathed. In the mad dash, I caught a glimpse of people sitting in gutters and children playing in filth, while others looked hungry and hopeless. My stomach churned. Here we were on our way to the Mandarin Oriental Hotel. A clean and classy suite would soon be our home for the week, and we were passing by broken people who were helpless and homeless. These very people could be coming to the crusade to receive healing. I wanted to stop the car and get out and walk on the sidewalk. Somewhere deep inside, I felt confused and angry. *What's wrong with this picture?* I wondered.

As quickly as the question popped up in my mind, it was gone. If I hadn't known any better, I would have thought I was starting to sound like one of those news critics from NBC who always hated on my uncle. Rationalizations kicked in. *These people are in need. We meet their need. They go home blessed with hope and healing. We go home blessed for providing the hope and healing.* And that settled that. I could breathe again.

We made a brief stop to visit the crusade grounds, engaged in some aggrandizing conversations with local government officials, and passed several of the 120 large billboards placed throughout the city. The words "Pray for India Rally" sprawled across the billboard with Uncle Benny's face peering down upon onlookers. Soon we arrived at the hotel and it was time to rest. I had no idea of the historical moment that was about to happen.

By Friday night of that week, it was time for the crusade to begin.

Estimations varied from 800,000 to 1.3 million people in attendance the first night in Mumbai. With two more services in the crusade, we'd crush the million-person mark. Standing on the stage looking out over the assembly took my breath away. The crowd faded on the horizon because of how vast it was. After the choir started to sing the opening songs, I made my way off to the side of the stage.

Just then one of the crusade directors pulled up in a golf cart. "Costi, jump in!" he called. "We're going to drive the length of the crowd."

I got in as quickly as I could. The crowd was like a sea of ants. How in the world were we going to get through it all? I checked my watch and started the timer. Forty-five minutes later, we had navigated more than two dozen sound systems spaced out across the grounds with large projected television screens, and had woven our way through one million people along a path that ran parallel to the fields. Estimates put the total number for all of the services at more than four million people.

The Sick and Diseased

The population of Mumbai is around eighteen million people, and 20 percent attended the crusade. The hundreds of thousands who came were the most desperate of the desperate. During one of the services, my father let me join him in the area where the sick gathered to receive prayer. My uncle never went into these areas to lay hands on people himself because he had to run the service from the stage, but the ministry hired workers and enlisted volunteers to pray for the sick and look for potential testimonies to bring onto the platform. My dad was one of those employed to run the healing lines. As we walked through the aisles of sick and diseased people, my adrenaline fired. *How in the world can this be happening? Look at these people!*

The thoughts ran through my nineteen-year-old mind, and I couldn't shake the emotion. Tears streamed down my face as I wondered, *God, where are you? Please heal these people!* A blind child was desperately clutching his mother. Paralyzed hopefuls lay in the dirt or sat in makeshift wheelchairs, while others screamed to be prayed for as they agonized in pain. Some had nice medical equipment, but most looked like something you'd see in a movie—except this wasn't staged. It was reality, and the cameras were focused on the beautiful music and the happy stories told from the stage.

There, in a dark corner of Mumbai, I came face to face with a kind of despair I had never seen before. Leaving the ivory tower left me confused. From the gold palace in Dubai, to the crowd of sick and diseased people. My heart still races describing it. We were supposed to heal these poor souls. Why weren't they being healed? These children were supposed to grow up healthy, wealthy, and full of joy. Why couldn't we just help them all right now? That's what we promised, but not what we delivered.

Don't Put God in a Box

Whether I was witnessing thousands of people speaking in tongues without interpretation, or talking with someone from our inner circle who admittedly faked being slain in the Spirit by flying through the air at the wave of the white jacket (to make it look *really* powerful), questions were quenched by several key phrases. The first of which was, "Don't put God in a box." What this means is that if you didn't accept or agree with what was being taught or the antics that were being displayed, you shouldn't assume God wasn't behind such a thing or you could be found guilty of limiting God. Sometimes it seemed like we were being forced to accept insanity. Other times, what we witnessed was so opposed to the Bible it seemed like we were rewriting it altogether!

One Sunday during a healing service, we declared everyone healed, even though half the people were still sick when they left. *Don't put God in a box. We must believe something is true even if our eyes don't see it.* At another service, people were being ripped out of wheelchairs left and right and barely limping across the stage. An elderly woman winced in pain as she was forced to walk in front of the crowd and told, "Just move your legs in faith! Don't limit God with your unbelief! He is healing you right now!" She was still in her wheelchair the next time I saw her. *What's the problem here?* I wondered. *Did God really just curse that old lady back into her wheelchair because she was boxing him in with her weak faith?* During another service, a woman had a brace ripped off her body as she screamed in pain. The pastor shouted, "That's the devil of infir-mity coming out of her!"

Our faith healing heroes of the past had set the course for this behavior, so I wasn't about to go against them. Smith Wigglesworth, a British evangelist who ministered in the early 1900s, was the pioneer of using physical violence as a form of healing. He allegedly walked into a mortuary and threw a man's corpse up against a wall in an effort to raise him from the dead. While many of the more outlandish stories can't be verified, in one of his books, Wigglesworth admitted to beating on people to heal them and said he was attacking the devil in them.[2]

I often cringed at the stories I heard about Wigglesworth, but I was intrigued by the risks he'd taken. That risk factor, I was told, was the hallmark of a faithful Christian. We even celebrated Wigglesworth's violent antics. "Sometimes, you need to throw away your medicine, fire your doctor, and dare God to heal you!" my uncle would roar from the platform. "Wigglesworth had crazy faith!" my father would tell me as he explained the auda-cious moves we needed to make to tap into God's power.

Were we abusing people? Were the heroes of our faith false teachers we'd followed into infamy? Or was I guilty of putting God in a box because I doubted what appeared to be insanity?

---

2   In one of his books, Wigglesworth explained his controversial assaults on sick people: "There are some times when you pray for the sick and you are apparently rough. But you are not dealing with a person, you are dealing with the satanic forces that are binding that person. Your heart is full of love and compassion to all, but you are moved to a holy anger as you see the place the devil has taken position in the body of the sick one, and you deal with his position with a real forcefulness" (Smith Wigglesworth, *Ever Increasing Faith* [Springfield, MO: Gospel Publishing House, 1924], 135–36).

Don't Touch the Lord's Anointed

We loaded into the cars as the California sun burst through the marine layer coming off the ocean. It was a typical Monday morning for the Hinn family as we joined my uncle on a drive to Beverly Hills for some shopping, meeting first at his home on the Pacific. I got in the driver's seat of his G-Class Benz. I was the chauffeur on this day. The rest of our entourage, about four men (including our executive protection team), got into the chase vehicle. They were to follow closely behind, ensure we could change lanes with ease, and provide protection if we were stalked by the paparazzi.

As I started the car and pulled out from Uncle Benny's driveway, the sound of a familiar voice began to play through the speakers. It was Kathryn Kuhlman—we'd listen to her and reminisce about her powerful ministry in days gone by. This famous leading lady of the televangelist circuit loved to spend donations on the finer things in life. She was a staple in our ears and the model for our ministry, both on the stage and in the stores.

Within an hour or so, we were pulling up on Beverly Street, just parallel to world-famous Rodeo Drive. After a brief walk, we spent some time in Monsieur Bijan's store (by appointment only), where a single suit can easily cost upward of ten thousand dollars. He designs some of the finest clothing in the world, and the prices reflect his unique style and rare talent. Presidential photos are scattered throughout the store. This was where the richest of the rich and the leading men of our nation shopped. I'd been here more times than I could count and had never felt an ounce of guilt.

Suddenly, for a split second, my mind flashed back to certain criticisms I'd heard about our ministry. *Is this what they're referring to?* I wondered. *Should a pastor be spending more money on clothing in a single shopping spree than the average annual salary of the people he's preaching to? How many sick and desperate people did it take to pay for that suit?* I needed to be careful. Such thoughts could get me in trouble with God for questioning an anointed leader.

Our visit concluded and purchases made, it was off to visit Leon's Jewelry for watch shopping. Photos lined the walls of celebrities who wore his watches at awards shows in Hollywood. On this particular day, as I left with another diamond-encrusted watch, I asked myself, *What are we? Pastors? Celebrities? Both?* It just didn't add up. I was beginning to think that there was a difference between being well known for faithful ministry and behaving like this. *Shouldn't money be a tool for doing more ministry? I'm sure it's okay for a pastor to own a home and be paid an adequate salary to care for his family, but tens of millions of dollars are going into our houses, cars, jewelry, hotels, and shopping. Could the critics be at least just a little bit right?*

Those questions were strictly locked away in my mind, never to be voiced, as I remembered the last time I questioned our lifestyle. I could hear my family members' rebuke as they cautioned, "Touch not the Lord's anointed, Costi! Judge not lest you be judged also. In the same manner in which you judge, so too you will be judged!"

One sermon I heard went something like this: "When a man is anointed by God, don't touch him! Even if that man is a devil, the office he functions within is anointed. Don't speak against him or you'll be cursed!" I was caught between wondering whether this was the ultimate gag order or the divine decree of God. Was it possible that the family I loved was abusing people with their power and influence? And if so, shouldn't they be held accountable?

With no one to turn to, and no way to find answers—so I thought—silence and submission were my only options.

Unfulfilled Prophesies

Another aspect of the prosperity gospel is an emphasis on prophecy. I knew this side of our ministry quite well. People would fly in from all over the world to seek out prophetic wisdom from my father and uncles. Hanging on their every word, these desperate people based every decision they made on the prophecy given. We used a strategy we called shotgun prophecy, firing off numerous predictions in the hope that one of the prophecies might hit the target and we'd be considered accurate and reliable.

One day, while browsing at a Christian bookstore, I came across a thick book titled *The Confusing World of Benny Hinn*. Its authors spent many years putting together hundreds of quotes by my uncle, then biblically explaining why he was a heretic.

I sighed. Here go the Christian watchdogs again. I'd already heard the "Bible Answer Man" Hank Hanegraaff criticize my uncle on the radio. And I'd witnessed the mockery of friends at school as they pulled off their jackets and knocked each other down with them. I figured this was just another attempt by someone to slander my family. But something inside me was curious. I bought the book.

Up to that day, my confidence abounded, money was not a problem, and criticisms rolled off my shoulders because of the global influence my family was privy to. *Who cares what people say?* I would tell myself. *Our family is the most anointed in the world.* But as I stared at the book in my hands, it felt like it weighed one hundred pounds.

That night, my entire house was dark but for the reading light next to my bed. Alternating between my favorite yellow highlighter and a fine-tip pen, I pulled an all-nighter and devoured the book.

The thrust of the book taught that God does not take kindly to leaders going around lying to people in his name. Deuteronomy 18:21–22 specifically instructs the children of Israel not to trust or fear someone who falsely prophesies: "You may say in your heart, 'How will we know the word which the LORD has not spoken?' When a prophet speaks in the name of the LORD, if the thing does not come about or come true, that is the thing which the LORD has not spoken. That prophet has spoken it presumptuously; you shall not be afraid of him." Then the authors detailed a number of Uncle Benny's unfulfilled prophecies.

One unfulfilled prophecy stood out to me. The authors had gotten ahold of the cassette tape for the December 31, 1989, Sunday-night service. In the service, Uncle Benny prophesied, "The Lord also tells me to tell you that in the midnineties, about '94 or '95, no later than that, God will destroy the homosexual community of America." Hinn's declaration was greeted with loud applause from his congregation. Uncle Benny continued, "But he will not destroy it with what many minds have thought him to be. But he will destroy it with fire. And many will turn and be saved, and many will rebel and be destroyed."[3]

As I read, my mind exploded with shock, but denial quickly

---

3   G. Richard Fisher and M. Kurt Goedelman, *The Confusing World of Benny Hinn: A Call for Discerning the Ministry and Teaching of the Popular Healing Evangelist* (St. Louis: Personal Freedom Outreach, 2013), 232.

rushed in. I began to reason, frantically trying to process emotions and facts. *God was going to burn all gay people by 1995? It has been more than twenty years since then, and we've yet to see fire come down from heaven on them.*

This was no typical Christian viewpoint on marriage being defined as between one man and one woman, nor was it one of those angry demands for homosexuals to repent. This was an unfulfilled prophecy, which meant Uncle Benny would be considered a false prophet by the Bible's standard.

I remembered hearing my uncle tell us that God frequently changed his mind about certain prophecies if people prayed hard enough. *Maybe that's what happened?* I reasoned, trying to understand why his prophecy hadn't been fulfilled.

When I told my father about what I'd read, he chided me. "Oh, please, Costi, that is so old. Those Pharisees have nothing better to do. Your uncle is a man of God. Ignore that stuff." His response held my questioning at bay for a short while. But there was no denying it. Something fishy was going on.

My whole life was in danger of falling apart. But I wasn't ready to face what that would mean. How could I ever stand up to an empire without being crushed? Was I supposed to confront my family? What would my father say if I finally pushed back hard enough to make waves? Would I lose the people I loved? End up homeless? Dead? How would I survive?

Questions swirled in my mind over the course of several years, and eventually the answers came in the most unlikely ways. Soon there would be a beautiful girl and helpful pastors, but it all started with a Baptist baseball coach who taught me more about life than about baseball. He planted the seeds of gospel truth down deep in my soul.

6

Don't Let Those Baptists Brainwash You

If God is not sovereign,
then God is not God.

—R. C. SPROUL

After two years of working for Uncle Benny, in the fall of 2004 I enrolled in a California community college for some much needed study. I also began to play baseball again. Before I knew it, my sophomore year was in full swing and I was having a great season. During practice one day, the coach called me over to ask where I wanted to transfer. You can't play all four years of baseball in a community college, so a transfer to a university was the next logical step. Some schools had called asking about me for recruiting purposes, but the coach wanted to know where I wanted to go. I blurted, "Dallas Baptist University."

At the time, DBU was a small division 1 school, but it was building a solid baseball program. Most of all, I thought it would be a good fit because it seemed like a great place to get away from family for a while. It would appease my parents, too, because it was a Christian school. Even though my parents preferred I go to Oral Roberts University (another division 1 Christian school), they understood my not wanting to go there after my sister and cousin had already done so.

Looking back, I realize God was orchestrating his plan for my life and mercifully putting me in a position to be exposed to the truth. But just a few weeks from my move to Dallas, the warnings came thick and fast.

"Now, Costi, I want you to hear me on this. I am your father and you need to heed my counsel." My dad began "the talk" that night in a little Italian restaurant in Dana Point, California.

"Those people there in Dallas are Baptists. They teach some solid stuff, but in the end, they will lead you astray. They're all head knowledge with no heart. They have some truth, but no power behind it," he explained. "They grieve the Holy Spirit. Make sure you do not become like them."

"Relax, Baba, I can handle myself," I told him. (Baba is the name I call my father in Arabic.) "I'm going there to play baseball, not to become some stuffy Baptist. It doesn't matter what they do or say. I know who I am, where I come from, and what I am there to do."

"Just don't lose the anointing on your life," he concluded. "Your mother and I are very concerned."

About that time, the head coach from DBU who had recruited

me called to tell me he had taken a job with Nebraska, but I'd be in good hands with his replacement, the assistant coach, Dan Heefner. I wasn't pleased. I had enjoyed a good connection with the coach whom I'd had my recruiting visit with, and I had no idea what was in store under a new coaching regime. *Oh well*, I thought. *A new coach, a new college—here we go!*

What Baptists Think of the Prosperity Gospel

You may be wondering why my going to a Baptist university was such a big deal to my family.

Not to put too fine a point on it, but Baptists *hate* the prosperity gospel. That is not to say they hate the *people* preaching it, but it is to say they hate the content because it smears the true gospel. Russell Moore, president of the Ethics and Religious Liberty Commission of the Southern Baptist Convention, has been quoted numerous times repudiating the prosperity gospel. He, along with preacher and civil rights activist John Perkins, decried the prosperity gospel as especially damaging to African Americans in the US. Perkins called out African-American prosperity preacher Creflo Dollar (yes, his last name really is Dollar) for trying to raise sixty-five million for his own private jet when that money could have established an accredited African-American evangelical school. Perkins called the prosperity gospel "almost witchcraft," and Moore doubled down on that statement by flat-out calling it witchcraft.[1]

---

1   Russell Moore, "How the Prosperity Gospel Hurts Racial Reconciliation," DesiringGod .org, April 25, 2015, https://www.desiringgod.org/articles/how-the-prosperity-gospel-hurts -racial-reconciliation.

Albert Mohler, president of the Southern Baptist Convention's flagship school, Southern Baptist Theological Seminary, is never one to back down from speaking the truth in a public forum. He minces no words about the prosperity gospel when he says:

Prosperity theology is a False Gospel. Its message is unbiblical and its promises fail. God never assures his people of material abundance or physical health. Instead, Christians are promised the riches of Christ, the gift of eternal life, and the assurance of glory in the eternal presence of the living God. In the end, the biggest problem with prosperity theology is not that it promises too much, but that it promises far too little. The Gospel of Jesus Christ offers salvation from sin, not a platform for earthly prosperity. While we should seek to understand what drives so many into this movement, we must never for a moment fail to see its message for what it is—a false and failed gospel.[2]

Conrad Mbewe, the bold African preacher and pastor of Kabwata Baptist Church in Lusaka, Zambia, has been clear on the prosperity gospel for years. Since he stepped into the pulpit at KBC, he has witnessed the prosperity gospel take over his continent. Mbewe calls the prosperity gospel "religious fraud."[3]

Clearly, the Baptists do not take kindly to prosperity charlatans raking in the big bucks off the backs of the poor, nor do they approve of deceiving people with a false version of Jesus.

---

2 Albert Mohler, "It Promises Far Too Little—The False Gospel of Prosperity Theology," Albert Mohler.com, August 18, 2009, https://albertmohler.com/2009/08/18/it-promises-far-too-little-the-false-gospel-of-prosperity-theology/.

3 Conrad Mbewe, "Our Criminal Evangelical Silence," Conrad Mbewe.com, October 11, 2012, http://www.conradmbewe.com/2012/10/our-criminal-evangelical-silence.html.

Enter: the Hinn kid rolling in a Hummer onto the campus of the Southern Baptist Convention endorsed school, Dallas Baptist University. What could go wrong?

Cordial but Not Condoning

The fall of 2007, I walked into my New Testament Survey class and sat down in the back row. My first professor at DBU was Dr. Mike Milburn. He began taking roll on the first day.

With a Texas twang, he said, "Costi Hinn," and looked up.

"Here," I muttered.

"You kin to Benny?" he quipped. It sounded more like Binny with that southern accent.

"Yes, sir," I said, while shifting in my chair hoping he would just move on to the next name.

"Well, I suppose I ought to watch my mouth a little when we get to certain parts of the class material, now, shouldn't I?" He chuckled.

I smiled uncomfortably, not knowing what to say.

"I'm just kidding, relax," he reassured me with a warm smile.

As we plowed through the New Testament, Dr. Milburn never once mistreated me, made a disrespectful comment, or pushed his agenda onto me. He did, however, teach the Bible unapologetically, sparking in me a deep interest in Scripture. Along with presenting solid material, Dr. Milburn told stories, making the class time fly by. His model of ministry can be summed up in one word: faithfulness. Until his retirement in 2016, he pastored the same church in Burleson, Texas, for twenty-nine years. A man of integrity and consistency, he was celebrated by the local newspaper for all the work he had done in that community.[4] That picture of longevity and faithfulness without any controversy over integrity or financial exploits was one I had never encountered. My experience in that first classroom serves as a perfect illustration of the clear truth I was taught and the kindness I was shown at Dallas Baptist University.

Came for Baseball but Got More Bible

My New Testament class wasn't the only place where I encountered a different gospel than the one I'd grown up in. The baseball program also exemplified the school's faith commitment. The team went on a missions trip to Guatemala during fall break, conducted inner city baseball clinics in Oak Cliff (a nearby community with various needs), and engaged in discipleship, discipleship, then more discipleship. We had a Bible study group called The Oaks, where we had to memorize Scripture and meet with our accountability partners. There was also a midweek discipleship study with the entire team every Wednesday at 1:00 p.m. right before our official practice. Coach Heefner taught us from the Bible on topics like marriage, dating, sexual purity, and character.

I can honestly say that most of my teammates lived out their faith in an incredible way. Unfortunately, I was really good at saying all the right things but living hypocritically. Still, the program kept trucking along, challenging and shaping me. With each day of getting better on the field, we were inundated with

---

4   "Milburn 'Understood What People Needed': Pastor Retires after Twenty-Nine Years at Burleson's First Baptist Church," Burleson Star, August 23, 2016, https://www.burlesonstar.net/news-local-news/milburn-understood-what-people-needed.

spiritual principles off the field. Hard work was a nonnegotiable. If you weren't fifteen minutes early, you were late, and if you weren't a team player, you were toast. It was one for all, and all for one. We were a team, and Coach Heefner was the glue that held it together—only he wasn't relying on himself, he was relying on God.

After a six-week study on biblical marriage and relationships, he squared up with all of us right there in the locker room. "Understand this, guys! Everything starts with you. Being a man is taking responsibility for your actions and for your families one day. Real men don't blame their wives for their own failures and shortcomings. They own up and lead out by example."

I remember the sound of his voice to this day. His usual calm and collected demeanor was as unwavering as ever.

"And remember this—the habits you are forming and living with during these years will go with you into the years ahead. Make sure you understand that. What you become now will shape you for the rest of your life. Your future wife and your future family are going to be joined to, and influenced by, who you choose to be."

Coach went on to tell us stories about the integrity and character of big leaguers like Ben Zobrist (who was the World Series Most Valuable Player for the Chicago Cubs in 2016). Ben happened to be Coach Heefner's brother-in-law and a DBU baseball alum, so Coach knew him well. Coach told us about some of the strategies that Ben used when on the road in the major leagues to remain above reproach. He was an example of a real Christian man, committed to doing the right thing even when no one was looking. Stories like this always resonated with us because we could relate to fellow athletes who were in the trenches of temptation.

Conviction tied my stomach into knots. I was a total hypocrite. I really wanted what Coach described when he talked about a godly marriage, a godly life, and godly character, but how? My life looked good on the outside, but on the inside I was a mess. I was memorizing all of the Scriptures we were assigned. I could rattle off 1 John 1:9, 1 Corinthians 10:13, Galatians 2:20, 2 Corinthians 5:17, John 5:24, and more. I was doing my Bible reading plan, landing on the dean's list for good grades, and working hard on the field and in the weight room, but my heart wasn't changing. I wanted the other life, but it didn't seem possible to have it without leaving everything I had ever known. *Is this really how Christianity works?* I wondered. *Or is this the Baptist brainwashing Dad warned me about? Maybe they really are ruining me!*

The Seed of Sovereignty

It was the words of Coach Heefner during a warm afternoon scrimmage that planted the seed of truth that eventually decimated my belief system. That afternoon was particularly tense. We always treated scrimmages like a real game, so in our minds, this wasn't practice; it was a game. But what made things really tense was that a New York Yankees scout had seated himself in the stands right behind home plate. Scouts visited practices to see players they were interested in, and our team happened to have numerous future professional players and multiple big leaguers. Victor Black went on to play for the Mets, Brandon Bantz eventually got the callup with the Mariners, and Ryan Goins became a fan favorite with the Blue Jays before ending up with the Royals, and now the Phillies. With so many talented players on the team, it was still unnerving every time a scout showed up. Put on a show, and a player could end up drafted. Disappoint, and they might cross you off their watch list. Coach understood the pressure we were under, so he turned our attention to a higher level of thinking: biblical truth.

"Bring it up." He called us together for a quick huddle. "Now listen, I don't want you getting all worried about scouts. We have one job today, and that's to play this game for the glory of God. Scouts aren't in control. God is sovereign."

He then quoted Proverbs 21:1: 'The king's heart is like channels of water in the hand of the LORD; He turns it wherever He wishes.' God controls kings, he controls scouts, and he is in control of your life. He is sovereign! Now go out there, have some fun, and play the game."

My mind clicked from baseball to the bigger picture. My prosperity gospel theology was causing a glitch in my ability to process his statement. *What is he talking about? What does that even mean? So the scout is just a puppet? Our future is already set? My faith controls nothing? We are supposed to have faith for what we want and then God will just do it. Sovereignty of God? Okay, Coach, now how do I get sovereignty to work in my favor? By having enough faith! That's how. Guys just need to have enough faith to get drafted and they will. End of story.*

Maybe Coach wasn't as smart as I thought he was. Maybe I could teach him a thing or two about having faith and speaking things into existence. My locker and the parking lot outside the baseball stadium held all the evidence I needed. Sitting pretty in my locker was my ten-thousand-dollar limited edition Breitling watch. Sitting in the parking lot was my eighty-thousand-dollar Hummer, covered with chrome and loaded with TVs. Did the sovereignty of God provide that for this college kid? Nope! Faith did. Or so I thought.

An Open Life and an Open Bible

The aftermath of the sovereignty-of-God bomb soon subsided, but I would feel its effects later. For the remainder of my time at DBU, life was full of friendships, baseball, and witnessing Coach Heefner's life on and off the field.

At Thanksgiving, Coach invited all of the players who weren't going home to join him and his family for dinner, and several other players and I took him up on his offer. You can learn a lot about someone by visiting them at home. Throughout the afternoon and evening, I was amazed by the normalcy of Coach's home life and the consistency he exhibited. Even his wife and sons reflected Christ and had fun doing it! At one point, his sons pulled out some foam swords for a duel, and a brief timeout for a rough-and-tumble injury to the youngest boy was about as scandalous as it got. *Nobody is perfect, but this guy is the real deal,* I realized. Coach's wisdom poured out as the late afternoon turned to evening. He told us about the books he was reading, the book of the Bible he was memorizing (yes, an entire book), and even shared some of his parenting strategies for raising boys. All in all, his life was different from any life I had ever seen. There was no hypocrisy, no abuse of power or cheating the system, and no Scripture twisting.

Graduation came in 2009. The Dallas Baptist chapter of my life closed, and California called me home for the next stage of my life. I planned to take a job offer as an athletic trainer working with professional and college athletes. Aside from that, I had a desire to get into ministry work. Even though I still held to my belief system, after my time at DBU, I had an urge to be different, but I was still steeped in sin and in the prosperity gospel lifestyle. However, things were about to take an unpredictable turn.

Very soon the sovereignty of God was going to turn my world upside down.

The Sovereignty of God versus the Prosperity Gospel

It's important that we take a moment here to understand what it means that God is sovereign. For the Christian, believing that God is sovereign is one thing, but living in light of that truth can sometimes feel like a doctrinal wrestling match, particularly if you've been raised in the prosperity gospel.

The Bible clearly teaches that "our God is in the heavens; He does whatever He pleases" (Ps. 115:3). Paul, under the guidance of the Holy Spirit, told the Christians in Ephesus that God "works all things after the counsel of His will" (Eph. 1:11). When Job was going through hell on earth—losing his health, wealth, and even his children—his response to God after questioning him was not to curse him but to submit to his sovereignty. In an unprecedented response to the worst suffering a person can bear, Job said to God, "I know that You can do all things, and that no purpose of Yours can be thwarted. . . . Therefore I have declared that which I did not understand, things too wonderful for me, which I did not know. . . . I have heard of You by the hearing of the ear; but now my eye sees You; therefore I retract, and I repent in dust and ashes" (Job 42:2–3, 5–6).

After going through everything that he went through, Job questioned God but quickly realized there were things in life he might never fully understand. He took solace in knowing that God was in control of the outcome and was sovereign in the midst of his pain.

Some may ask, "If God is sovereign, then are we all just puppets on his heavenly strings?" The answer is a resounding no! God's sovereignty does not negate our responsibility or our free will to make choices. This is a divine tension that we must be content to live in because it's exactly as the Bible describes it. The glorious doctrine of God's sovereignty and the reality of our free will should not confuse us; rather, it should humble us into a greater understanding of our position. God is sovereign, infinite, and the sustainer of all things (Rom. 11:36). We are human, finite, and have been provided the freedom to exercise our will on earth and choose this day whom we will serve (Josh. 24:14–15). If we choose to serve our appetites and indulge in nothing but our pleasures, we will reap the outcome of those selfish choices. If we choose to submit to the sovereign God of the universe to do things his way, we will reap the outcome of those obedient choices.

The question may also naturally arise, "If God is sovereign, then why do bad things happen to good people?" The truth is, God's sovereignty is not in any way put in jeopardy when bad things happen to good people. It may never be an easy pill to swallow, but the Bible shows us clearly that even when evil appears to have won, God's ultimate purposes are being served.

The story of Joseph, told in Genesis 37–47, is one to keep close to your heart whenever questions arise in the midst of your pain. Joseph was one of twelve brothers and his father's favorite, and his brothers got jealous. They threw him into a pit, sold him into slavery, and told their father he was dead. Over the years that followed, Joseph was falsely accused of rape and even tossed into prison. One injustice after another. Was he ever going to catch a break? Still, he took each shot with integrity and held fast to his trust in God. Eventually he was released from prison, and in reward for his character and his trust in God, he became the Egyptian Pharaoh's righthand man! He was put in charge of food storage and distribution during a seven-year famine, and people from neighboring lands traveled great distances to buy food from Egypt.

One day, guess who showed up? Yes, those same brothers who had sold him out! It had been so many years, they didn't recognize him. After briefly toying with them (what brother wouldn't in that situation?), Joseph revealed his identity. The brothers begged for forgiveness, declaring they would be his servants. Joseph, having learned to trust in the sovereignty of God, said this in response: "Do not be afraid, for am I in God's place? As for you, you meant evil against me, but God meant it for good in order to bring about this present result, to preserve many people alive" (Gen. 50:19–20). How's that for perspective? Joseph knew that no matter what evil had taken place, in the end, God would work it out for good.

Famous nineteenth-century preacher Charles Spurgeon often preached about the sovereignty of God because it is one of the most important doctrines for the Christian. That God is sovereign means that he is supreme and all powerful and possesses complete authority. For those who are aware of their great need for God, the doctrine of sovereignty is a soft place to rest their weary souls, letting go and letting God. What good would it be if we were put in control anyway? To think that I am the master of my destiny and the ruler of my world is a burden the prideful side of my humanity longs to bear, but it is far too heavy to carry. That God is sovereign means he will one day wipe away every tear and right every wrong. There will be a short time on earth in which turmoil and pain seem to run rampant, but our lives are but specks compared with eternity. An infinite number of years in heaven will provide healing, riches, glory, and, best of all, life with Jesus. No matter what we face in this life, God is in control. We can trust in his promises for a better future.

Arthur Pink reminds us that the sovereignty of God is rarely preached today, though it should be talked about far more. Perhaps we despise the notion that someone other than ourselves is in control. Or perhaps we find this belief uncomfortable because it resolves to trust God in the midst of our deficient answers. He writes, "The sovereignty of God is an expression that once was generally understood. It was a phrase commonly used in religious literature. It was a theme frequently expounded in the pulpit. It was a truth which brought comfort to many hearts, and gave virility and stability to Christian character. But, today, to make mention of God's sovereignty is, in many quarters, to speak in an unknown tongue."[5]

R. C. Sproul explains that "sovereignty is a divine attribute confessed almost universally in historical Christianity" and that "if God is not sovereign over the entire created order, then he is not sovereign at all."[6]

The sovereignty of God matters to Christianity, and we could go as far as to say that it is un-Christian to deny the sovereignty of God. The prosperity gospel certainly denies the sovereignty of God to the extent that it demeans God to the position of a puppet and elevates man to the position of a puppet master who makes confessional demands by faith. It does this by considering faith as a force and God as the one who must respond to our faith. This

---

5 Arthur Pink, The Sovereignty of God (Dublin: First Love Publications, 2017), 29.

6 R. C. Sproul, What Is Reformed Theology? (Grand Rapids: Baker, 1997), 28–29.

is a heretical twisting of true faith. The Bible describes true faith and right confession as:

- The way to come clean to God about our sin (1 John 1:9).
- The way to surrender our lives to Jesus Christ (Rom. 10:9).
- The way to please God (Heb. 11:6).
- The way to be justified before a righteous God (Rom. 5:1).
- The way to approach God for wisdom and guidance (James 1:5).
- The way to be confident in the promises of God to come (Heb. 11:1).
- The way we live in light of Christ's sacrifice for us (Gal. 2:20).

None of these examples or the plethora of other passages throughout Scripture declare that faith and confession are the means by which God can be tapped for guaranteed health and wealth. He is sovereign; we are not.

Conversely, the prosperity gospel takes the sovereignty of God and tosses it aside, claiming that we can control the God of the universe. In the most arrogant claim that humans could make, prosperity preachers declare that our mouths control our money, and much more. They preach that:

- God wants you to be healthy. You just need to confess and believe for it.
- God wants you to be wealthy. You just need to confess and believe for it.
- God wants your life to be comfortable and easy. Your confession controls your outcomes.

- God wants you to have everything you need. Your negativity is your problem.
- God already sent Jesus to die for your abundant life. Your faith is the problem.
- God already sent Jesus to die for that job promotion to be yours.
- God already sent Jesus to pay for your debt so you can live debt free.

In the prosperity gospel, these are all earthly promises. If you say those sentences out loud, you can almost hear Joel Osteen's voice coming through each one. He, and the rest of the prosperity preachers across the world, will tell you that if you want something right now, then you need to confess it, believe it, and, of course, pay money for it. Sure, they'll tell you, Jesus is the way to heaven (John 14:6), but he didn't die merely to give you heaven to come. He died to give you riches today!

In his New York Times bestselling book, Joel Osteen writes, "Perhaps God has whispered something to your heart that seems totally impossible. It may seem impossible for you to ever be well again, or impossible for you to get out of debt, to get married, to lose weight, to start that new business. In the natural, physical realm, all the odds are against you; you don't see how it could happen. But if you're going to see those dreams come to pass, you have to get your mouth moving in the right direction and use your words to help you develop a new image on the inside. . . . Don't merely use your words to describe your situation; use your words to change your situation."[7]

---

7   Joel Osteen, Become a Better You: Seven Keys to Improving Your Life Every Day (New York: Free Press, 2007), 113–14.

Paula White, a world-renowned prosperity preacher and presidential advisor to Donald Trump, claims to know exactly why
Jesus came to earth. It wasn't to reconcile you to God the Father.
It wasn't merely to pay for sin and provide the eternal riches and
glory of heaven to the poor, the rich, and the broken. He came
to make you healthy and wealthy! In her book *Living the Abundant
Life: Why Not Me? Why Not Now?* she boldly asserts, "Prosperity
means: welfare, well-being; affluence (wealth); success; thrift,
roaring trade; good fortune, smiles of fortune; blessings; and
a godsend. . . . Jesus said, 'I come that you would have abundant life, that you would enjoy life.' He didn't say, 'You have to
wait to get to heaven before you will be blessed.' God came to
give me abundant life. . . . How do I begin to live the abundant
life of Christ? . . . You cannot be a non-tither and have God's
breakthrough."[8]

This twisting of the Bible makes God a cosmic banker in
charge of dispensing your wishes. It makes Jesus' death on the
cross simply a transaction to provide an earthly reward of fancy
cars, perfect health, and expanding bank accounts. If it were that
easy, then why doesn't every single person who confesses Jesus
Christ as Savior and Lord suddenly see their pockets fill with cash?
Why isn't their cancer healed when they repent of their sins and
confess Jesus as their loving Redeemer? If the sovereignty of God
works only to provide health and wealth, and Jesus died to provide an abundant life for all, then why are the prosperity preachers
the only ones driving Bentleys and living in multi-million-dollar
New York penthouses?

---

8 Paula White, *Living the Abundant Life: Why Not Me? Why Not Now?* (Tampa: Paula White
Ministries, 2003), 56–57.

When we get the sovereignty of God wrong, we get God wrong. When we get the abundant life wrong, we get Jesus wrong. When we get faith and confession wrong, we get salvation wrong.

Why is that a huge deal? Because all roads that the prosperity gospel paves lead to hell.

7

Marriage and Ministry: A Divinely Appointed Disaster

In the infinite wisdom of the Lord of all the earth, each event falls with exact precision into its proper place in the unfolding of His divine plan.

—B. B. WARFIELD

She drove a Toyota Yaris. I drove a Hummer. She had worked since age sixteen. The only job I ever had involved traveling on a Gulfstream jet. Her parents were hardworking blue-collar folk. We were prosperity gospel ballers. We might as well have been from two different planets. But soon this girl named Christyne would be coming down an aisle in a white dress and I'd be fighting back the tears as she got closer. Before that moment, however, God would allow some major mishaps to bring me into a new season of life and true saving faith.

Everything I Ever Wanted, Everything I Need

It was a gorgeous September weekend in 2009 when my best friend at the time invited me to join him and his girlfriend at a country music festival in Lake Elsinore, California. It was taking place at a baseball stadium, so we thought it'd be fun to be on the field for the concert. He supplied me with a free ticket, and I offered to drive. His old white Honda Civic was a bit less comfortable than my Hummer.

The concert was a two-day event. We parked with thousands of other people, and I kept the back hatch of the Hummer open so we could hear the music blasting through my speakers. The only problem was that the car wasn't running, but the key was turned on—the battery eventually died. Figuring we would deal with it after the concert, we locked it up and went into the stadium. Not long after we sat down, I saw her.

Christyne was walking down the stairs and nearly reached her aisle when we caught each other's eyes. I smiled the biggest, cheesiest smile of my life. She gently smiled back, then quickly lowered her head and shuffled to her seat, sitting down with the girl she was with. I immediately began brainstorming. *How in the world am I going to talk to her?*

My buddy, noticing my interest, laughed at me. "What is wrong with you, Costi?" he teased.

"I don't know, man. I just have to meet that girl. There's something about her. She's beautiful! I want to get to know her." I had no idea why I suddenly was struck with this urge to meet her, except that it was the typical urge of a single guy who sees a beautiful girl and hopes to talk to her. But how do you start a conversation with someone you've never met?

"I got it! The Hummer is dead! I can ask them for a jump." I was elated with my failproof idea.

Before he could respond as a voice of reason, I was out of my seat and standing right next to her in the aisle. Stammering, I said, "Excuse me? I know this is random, but my car died in the parking lot earlier, and I was wondering if after the concert you gals could help me and my friends over there by giving us a jump?"

"Sure, no problem!" they said in unison.

"Thanks!" I walked back to my seat knowing I had only a couple of hours to figure out my next move.

A couple of hours later, the concert wrapped up and we all headed to the parking lot together. As we walked, the small talk began, and before I knew it, my buddy had discovered they had mutual friends, and everyone was talking and comfortable. The girl with Christyne was her sister.

We approached the Hummer and my buddy said, "Hey, Costi, try starting it first. Sometimes when a car sits for a while it will restart."

"Okay," I said. Turning to Christyne I quickly clarified, "Just so you know, if this thing starts, that whole 'my car died and I need a jump' thing was not just a line to meet you."

She laughed and playfully piped back, "Just turn the key and we'll see, mister!"

I reached in and turned the key. The engine roared to life. I was busted!

"Liar!" She pointed her finger, laughing.

"I kid you not—the battery really was dead," I defended myself, but to no avail.

Some thirty minutes of talking and teasing ensued. Finally, Christyne and her sister asked, "Are you guys coming back tomorrow for day two of the concert?"

"Yes, but we won't be here until the afternoon. She has to be at church all morning," I responded, gesturing toward my buddy's girlfriend.

Christyne's sister smiled. "Oh, you're church people? Well, you'll like her." She pointed to Christyne. "She's a little church girl too!"

I grinned. *She's a Christian! That settles it. I am totally asking if she'll let me take her to dinner.*

To ensure that I had her number, I offered some helpful advice. "Well, let's exchange numbers so we can all meet up tomorrow and find each other when we arrive." It worked. She agreed. Now, I just needed to muster up the courage to ask her to dinner.

After enjoying day two of the concert, we all stood in the parking lot preparing to say goodbye. Then I went for it. But before I did, her sister made a comment for good measure.

"Just so you know, my sister isn't impressed with your Hummer. She's not that type of girl." Her comment only increased my interest.

"May I take you to dinner this week? When are you free?" I asked Christyne.

"Every day this week I have school, then work. I get out of class in the afternoon, then go to my job at TGI Fridays until 11:00 p.m. So, no."

Undeterred, I said, "Okay, what are you doing Monday night?"

"School, then work."

I confidently marched onward while the onlookers winced, feeling the pain of my rejection but entertained by my hopeless efforts. "Tuesday?"

"School, then work."

My confidence suddenly shattered, I wasn't feeling so invincible. This Christian girl was not interested. Should I even try for Wednesday?

Then, rushing to my rescue, her sister interrupted. "She's free Wednesday!"

Everyone froze. I smiled. Done!

"Okay, Wednesday it is," Christyne reluctantly accepted. Later on I found out that she had to call her boss and change her shift because she was, in fact, not free on Wednesday. I still owe my sister-in-law for this one!

That Wednesday, I pulled up to her house after following my GPS for sixty miles wondering, *Where in the world am I?* She lived as far away from me as I could have imagined. But during our sushi date, I realized this was worth every bit of the 120-mile roundtrip trek. She was a newer Christian and was putting herself through a Christian college, going to school all day, then working until the wee hours of the morning. She attended a non-prosperity gospel church on her own, had a few close friends, and was happily independent. She paid all her bills, was highly conservative, and had little interest in dating. God must have been working in a sovereign way behind the scenes because this girl had no business wasting time on a prosperity gospel guy like me.

We went on a few more dinner dates, and soon, we went together to a church where I was more comfortable. It was a prosperity gospel church led by a TBN preacher my family thought highly of. Christyne wasn't exactly keen on everything about the church, but she was supportive of me. Around that time, someone suggested that she check the internet and research my uncle, offering words of caution about my family ties. To that she responded, "I'm not going to look at anything on the internet, because I don't want to judge Costi through that lens. I'll get to know him and decide for myself." I was instantly relieved.

She Shattered the Mold and My Theology

Some months went by, and during that time, I kept Christyne at arm's length from my family. They knew I was seeing someone, but I played it off like it wasn't anything serious. She was very different, and I assumed, perhaps wrongly, they would take exception to that. Everything we believed and everything I had ever been taught stood in direct contradiction to my relationship with her. She didn't speak in tongues, was not charismatic, and had no connection to my family of generationally anointed Christian leaders. The expectations were that I would most certainly marry someone who fit into those categories. Furthermore, she was an introverted, linear-thinking, blue-collar psych major. I had been taught that psychology is the enemy of faith and healing and that logical thinking is the antithesis to supernatural miracles and abundance. Based on all of that, God couldn't have picked a worse fit for a prosperity gospel royal family heir (which is what I was told I was!).

It had been prophesied over me from a young age that I was to be the next great anointed healer in the family. One "prophet" laid hands on my forehead after one of my uncle's crusades and declared that I was going to take the church to new heights and that millions of healings would take place by my hands. To date, I had never healed a single person, but the girl I was to marry was

supposed to fit the mold of such a ministry. I was always supposed to marry someone from our family's circle of friends. She'd
be a nice girl whose parents worshiped my last name. She'd rock a
Louis Vuitton, raise her hands in worship, speak in tongues daily,
and raise children named after our familial heroes in the faith. I
was supposed to be the next big thing, but all I was going to be
was the next big disappointment.

By early 2010, things caught up with me, and because of my
desire to marry Christyne, I had to face the music. Hoping to slip
past my parents' enormously high charismatic standards, I dropped
a little hint that it would be nice to introduce the girl I was seeing
to them. *Maybe they'll be cool about it,* I thought. I was wrong.

"Sounds good, that's fine," my parents responded after I
explained that I'd be inviting the girl over to meet them.

"She's a Christian, right?" one parent asked.

"Yes, of course."

"Is she Spirit filled?" they asked.

I knew what they meant: *Does she speak in tongues?* My blood
started to surge, adrenaline fired, and anxiety kicked in.

"C'mon! Don't start with that question. Yes, she's Spirit filled.
Does she speak in tongues or do things like we do? No. But that
doesn't mean she isn't Spirit filled. We all get the Holy Spirit when
we become Christians. I still remember that from a class at DBU."

Breathing heavily, my half-vetted theological rant over, I felt
like I was on the witness stand trying to convince a judge of my
innocence.

"Yes, we get the Holy Spirit when we're saved, but the evidence
of having the Holy Spirit is speaking in tongues. She's not Spirit
filled." The finality of their statement was like a dagger.

I nearly exploded with anger but held it in for fear of losing the chance to bring Christyne home to meet them. *How dare they say such things? They don't know her. She's amazing. If only they'd give her a chance. Why are tongues always such a huge deal breaker?* These questions surged through my mind like a flood.

We made it through meet-and-greet number one and a few small visits before eventually everyone got used to the idea that "Costi is dating an outsider." Everyone except for one sister, who had yet to meet Christyne because she lived in another state. One evening when this sister was visiting, she confronted me.

"She's not your wife, Cost." My sister described how God told her that this girl I was seeing was not my wife.

"You don't even know her," I argued.

"I don't need to know her. I know what God showed me."

By the fall of 2010, the pressure began to mount and the subjective "words from the Lord" continued from all angles. Perhaps at first they thought I was just casually dating this girl, but when it finally hit them that it was serious, the pushback increased a hundredfold.

"She's not your wife, Cost." The lecture began one night after I came home from a date with her. It was like deja vu all over again.

"If you marry her, you'll lose the anointing on your life. All it takes is a woman like that to ruin your faith. She's too dry. Not enough faith. She isn't like us."

It wasn't that Christyne didn't have faith for what she couldn't see, or that she was mean-spirited or rude. It was that she didn't necessarily fall at the feet of everything my family would say or preach. She was, understandably, cautious. And that caution cost her their approval at the time. She viewed the Bible as black and white. If the Bible said it, she'd believe it. We, on the other hand, twisted a lot of things the Bible said.

Christyne was a hard worker who viewed wealth as something that comes from working hard and having integrity. Someone could be extremely rich, but how they got rich and how they used their money was important if they said they were a Christian. Our California home, which she'd visited, was worth well over two million dollars. Our second home in Canada, she knew, was worth north of three million dollars. The cars in the garage were Mercedes. The car I drove was a Hummer. The watch I wore was a limited edition Breitling costing ten thousand dollars. The clothing we bought was made by the top designers in the world, and a meal at one of the restaurants we ate at weekly cost as much as her weekly paycheck. This would all be fine and dandy if we were real estate moguls or corporate CEOs. But we were in ministry—and preaching the prosperity gospel at that. She had every right to be cautious. While she didn't think that all pastors had to be poor, it didn't make sense to her that we lived like celebrities off of donations.

Finally, after more than a year of dating, I cowered in passivity and succumbed to believing that Christyne was bad for my ministry aspirations and the anointing on my life. I broke off the relationship. After telling her that she "wasn't my wife," I resolved to move on and make a decision that pleased my family and set my course toward powerful ministry.

It wasn't long, though, before I couldn't sleep. This girl was different.

Day after day, I pondered what to do. Questions raced through my mind, and I doubted my decision. What if she was the kind of woman I needed? Wasn't a strong, godly woman the kind I should marry? Since when should someone's heritage dictate their future? Just because she wasn't "our kind" didn't mean God couldn't change and grow her to be one of us. Perhaps she was a better person than all of us and we didn't realize it. Finally, I reached a breaking point. Mustering up all the guts I had, I chose Christyne, if she would still have me, and whatever consequences I suffered would be worth it—*she* was worth it.

I contacted her and pleaded with her to meet for me an impromptu lunch later that week. As I stared into her eyes across our table at the cafe, I told her I was so sorry for breaking up with her and I wanted a chance to make things right. She smiled patiently. Then she blew me away with grace and a kindness I didn't deserve.

"I understand, Costi." She paused. Her poise unwavering, she began sharing wisdom beyond her years. "Though I honestly didn't think you would ever come back to me, I was certain this was a lesson you needed to learn for yourself. The Lord has not called you to live a life that pleases your parents, me, or anyone else, for that matter. You need to marry who *you* want to marry. You need to do what God has called *you* to do. You need to live *your* life the way God has called *you* to live it, not the way your family tells you to live it."

With every emphasis she put on the "you" statements, my heart raced and filled with passion. Not mere passion for her (though I was ready to elope right then and there), but passion to live unapologetically based on my convictions. There were a lot of things I did and a lot of things I believed that were based on the family traditions and beliefs I held to. I had a lot to learn, but this woman was willing to go on that journey with me. *Wow! What a gift from God,* I thought.

Changes needed to occur in our relationship, and Christyne issued an ultimatum. If we got back together, we'd be going to "her church" now. During the breakup, she got involved with a church plant with one of her oldest friends (who also had become a Christian) and began serving in the children's ministry. She would take me back, but she would not go back to the prosperity gospel church.

It was an easy decision for me—I just wanted to be with her. Little did I know that this church plant and the relationships we formed there in just one year were the door God would use to rescue us from the godless empire I was attached to.

Like most young men lost in the eyes of a beautiful and godly woman, I got caught up in the moment but didn't fully realize what life would be like if what I was about to say came true. I said to her, "No matter the cost, I'm going to marry you and we will serve the Lord together. I'm called to be in the ministry, and I don't know exactly what that looks like, but I am going to be a preacher. I don't care what my family says or what pressure they put on me not to marry you. You are a gift from God and you are going to be my wife. We're in this together!"

Cue the sappy romance music and the flying hearts. Still, we'd have to work through the differences between her and my family, and figure out how to resolve the theological tensions that seemed to be surfacing more and more. I was still living in a theological fog myself, unsure what I even believed. Looking back, I know God was sovereignly ordering my steps. But at the time, I felt like I was all over the map.

Back to Canada

From June 2010 to June 2011, in the midst of the turbulence with Christyne and the relationship, I began flying up to Vancouver,

Canada, to preach at my father's church—Vancouver Christian Center. Though ignorant of the necessary steps for ministry training, I wanted to get involved at the church. Then around February 2011, I told Christyne I just couldn't fight off the compulsion to preach and help people any longer. I wanted to be in the ministry, not just flying up to Vancouver periodically like an itinerate speaker. I needed to be with the people—that's what I thought a real pastor should do. Assuring her I would save for a ring and make good on my promise to marry her and eventually move her up north before our wedding, I left her in California.

On June 15, 2011, I drove a U-Haul 1,300 miles north. It was goodbye California, hello Canada! Perhaps motivated by my renewed passion for the church he had left, my father decided to walk away from the home in California, reduce some travel with my uncle, and go all in with us on the church in Vancouver. It would be like the old days! My mother and younger sister moved as well. We were all together in ministry and back home where we belonged—in Vancouver with our church.

Upon arriving in Vancouver, I knew I had to hit the ground running. Though we were focused on the church, my dad started traveling on his own again and sporadically with Uncle Benny. I started preaching weekly, rotating out only occasionally when my father wanted a turn to preach when he was home. In the seven years we'd been gone, the crowd had dwindled to around thirty people, but soon it started to grow. Some families came back, a few young people joined, parents got excited, and the youth ministry kicked up once again. We moved from renting an old hotel ballroom to renting a modern movie theater. We launched a new website, revamped an old outreach ministry to the homeless community downtown, and started volunteer teams to motivate the congregation to serve.

Things were really looking up, but the biggest change was in the pulpit. I wasn't trying to be antithetical to the family theology, but I started preaching sermons based on the Bible. At one point, I preached a sermon on Job and how God allowed trials in his life but was still in control. Stories about suffering were foreign to our church, but it seemed right to preach a more balanced view on tough times. Everything was always so peachy and perfect in our theology. God always healed, sickness was never useful, and anything bad was the result of your lack of faith. I remember thinking, *Job's story is so different from what we teach, but it seems like it could help a lot of people who are waiting for God to heal them. Why not just go for it?*

Shortly after preaching the sermon, I visited a church member who was in the hospital with a serious sickness. Instead of offering the guarantee of healing or giving false hope, I found myself turning to the book of Job and reading portions of it to this young man. Something felt right inside, but I still remember the insecure feelings I had, wondering if I was letting him down by not being able to heal him.

While some things were starting to change, other things didn't until I learned the hard way. One Sunday, trying to be like my father, I did an altar call so I could lay hands on people. I invited everyone up front and said, "If you need a fresh anointing from God, come down here and I want to pray for you." Slowly they came. I began laying my hands on their heads. One enthusiastic woman was slain in the Spirit; everyone else was stiffer than a statue. A girl I grew up with in the church walked up to me afterward and said, "You don't have to lay hands on us to give us something fresh from God like your dad did. The preaching works just fine." *Whoa!* I thought. *Where did that come from?* But I just smiled and brushed it off for fear of being an accomplice to her controversial idea.

When it came to sermon preparation, all I knew was that my dad used to study on Saturdays for the sermon on Sunday. So I took on the "weekend warrior" method for preaching: study all day for one day, then go out there and preach on Sunday. I would spend all day studying my sermon text from the Bible. I had no books, so I did "research" on Google and used online biblical interpretation resources. By some miraculous means, the sermons actually made some sense, and it wasn't long before it was a regular occurrence to preach things like "We need to go back to the Bible!" and "God speaks to us through his Word!" People would nod in agreement.

After pulpit-pounding on one particular Sunday, I walked into church the next week and a woman named Melida, who had known me since I was a little boy, handed me a book and quietly said, "You're on the right track. This book will help you. Keep going." Her demeanor made me think I was receiving a scandalous gift!

I looked down to see a book titled *Church Awakening: An Urgent Call for Renewal* by Chuck Swindoll. *Wow. Looks serious,* I thought. *I should read it.* That evening I read the book in a single sitting, and God used it to put some serious cracks in my prosperity gospel foundation. In a section about "evil men and impostors" who deceive people (2 Tim. 3:13), Swindoll writes, "Pretty clear, isn't it? We have another descriptive term in English for these individuals: charlatans. Watch out for phonies! Why? Paul adds, '[They] will proceed from bad to worse. . . .' Don't be surprised by deception. Rather, anticipate it. Assume it. Stay realistic in your appraisal of these days. . . . Don't be fooled by any of the externals you see: persuasive speech . . . attractive brochures . . . celebrity endorsements . . . big crowds . . . persuasive logic . . . appealing personalities . . . even open Bibles! I need to talk straight with you. Not everyone who wears a collar and uses a Bible is to be trusted."[1]

Wow! This guy is intense. I pondered what it would be like to have that kind of boldness. To just tell it like it is and call people to live the truth. I had accepted the lies as the truth for so long, but it was starting to feel like there were people out there who knew something I didn't. Those things that Swindoll described in his book were eerily close to describing our family ministry. Could it be? Were we those phonies?

I was getting nearer to the truth than I had ever been, but the blinders weren't completely off my eyes. At the same time I was trying to fix my father's church, my family was trying to fix Christyne.

We Just Need to Fix Her

I tried to keep the peace, Christyne tried to say all the right things, but my family decided she could be fixed. Even though I assumed we were all going to live happily ever after and do ministry together, a few important things needed to happen first. Four experiences occurred from 2011–2012 that shook us up. Three supposedly were destined to seal the deal for Christyne and provide the spiritual upgrade she needed to bear the Hinn family name. The fourth was the biggest eye-opener of them all. All of

---

1   Chuck Swindoll, *Church Awakening: An Urgent Call for Renewal* (New York: Faith Words, 2010), 184–85.

these experiences deepened our convictions about the dangers of the prosperity gospel circles we ran in.

1. *"She needs to go to Uncle Benny's service."* It was Friday, April 22, 2011, and my uncle was holding a Good Friday communion service at the Honda Center in Anaheim, California—just one block from the cafe where Christyne and I reunited. I wasn't able to attend because I was preaching in Canada on a ministry trip. My parents thought my absence would be the perfect opportunity for some bonding time with Christyne. I presumed it would be helpful for her to go to have her own experience too. Though I had questions about some of our methods and teachings, I didn't think that made the entire thing worth calling false. I still held the view that we were elite, anointed Christian leaders. I just thought we needed some reform.

That night, numerous Hinn family members were present. Even TBN founder Paul Crouch, a family friend, attended. If ever there was a night for Christyne to get the Holy Spirit the way my family hoped, this was it!

Christyne was seated right in the front row, next to my mother. The television footage I watched afterward captured her repeating the prayers after my uncle, closing her eyes, and raising her hands. She did all the right things to have the right experience. If she spoke in tongues or was slain in the Spirit, or if my uncle prophesied wonderful things about her being my wife, we were set! Uncle Benny was the trump card in our world. No matter what had happened previously, if he signed off on our relationship, it sealed the deal.

"How did it go?" I asked as we caught up on the phone late that night.

"It was fine. The music was beautiful. Other parts were . . . interesting." I could hear the hesitation in her voice.

"What is it? Tell me. Did he pray for you? Did you fall? Were my parents nice to you?" I pressed for answers.

"Your parents were very nice. Your uncle was very kind as well. I got to meet him in the green room afterward. Also, when I arrived at the stadium, one of his security guards came out and parked my car for me. I was treated very well."

I knew her well enough to know I needed to ask questions to get more out of her.

"Okay, so what *wasn't* good about it?" I asked, hoping to draw out her critical thinking.

"I just felt like something was off. When your uncle called everyone up to be prayed for, the crowd poured to the front of the stage desperate to encounter the power of God. I thought we would all go up for prayer if it was supposed to be something authentic, but instead, all of the people who were 'important' who were sitting in the front including me and your mom—went to the side of the stage to avoid being crushed by the crowd and just watched as your uncle knocked people over. It came off like a show—that's all. It seems like if God's power had really been there, we all would have wanted to be touched by it, and there would have been a genuine effort to experience whatever it was we were being told about."

Her commentary was crippling. What was I supposed to say to that? She was right! If the service were really the access point to the power of God Almighty himself, wouldn't everyone—including my uncle—be champing at the bit to press in? Why did my uncle always stay in a safe zone on the platform, or only on rare occasions venture to the first rows? Why would there be a side section for the elite to avoid the crowd of commoners? I knew the side section of seats Christyne had referenced, because I'd sat there whenever I attended a crusade as a young boy.

After the service was over, my parents took her to meet Uncle Benny. They exchanged a brief hello, and my uncle said something nice like, "This is Costi's friend? Wow, what a pretty friend he has." And that was it. So much for sealing the deal. Maybe a different environment would produce a different experience.

2. *"She needs to come under your father's ministry."* One of the key teachings in the prosperity gospel is the culture of honor. Like many of the unique names given to certain teachings, it has other names too. Some call it culture of reverence as well. No matter the term, the meaning is always the same: people who wanted special anointing needed to come under a certain man's ministry. An anointed man of God is to be revered on an almost godlike level. This isn't merely the usual high respect for a pastor and love for our church leaders who feed our souls. This is doing anything and everything the man of God wants in order to get what you need. If you need a special physical or spiritual blessing, the man of God is the one who has to touch you.

When it came to getting Christyne to be anointed like us, there was no amount of praying I could do—it wasn't going to happen. The culture of honor meant that only one of the "generals" could do it. Even though I was going to be her husband, the general was the spiritual covering of sorts. Another term we used for the general was spiritual father. In this case, it would be my own father. He would need to sign off on Christyne by laying hands on her head publicly. She would need to fall backward (be slain in the Spirit), or else it would be a sign of her resistance to his authority. Like a cult leader having ultimate veto power, generals could end marriages before they even began, excommunicate people even when they'd done nothing wrong, and trump what the Bible said anytime by saying God told them something directly. They could also take whatever money they wanted because they were the ultimate authority.

On the Sunday Christyne was to be prayed for, we were both called up to the front of the church. There we stood as the music was brought to a crescendo. Then, as the soft sound of strings played in the background, my father whispered into the microphone, "Lift up your hands and receive his touch." Lifting our hands was a sign of surrender to God. And the touch was going to be my father's hand, but we believed God was touching us through him.

"Lord, fill her with your Spirit," he prayed as his hand pressed upon Christyne's head.

I began to cry but wasn't sure why. Maybe I wanted her to get whatever it was she needed to get so we could be together forever. Maybe I was finally releasing emotions I had held in for so long. Or maybe I subconsciously felt helpless as I watched the system force her into this situation. Before I could even blink, she was falling into the hands of one of the catchers and they were laying her gently on the ground. She looked stoic as I peered over at her. Within a minute or so, I was prayed for as well and fell backward, lying next to her on the floor. My father spoke a special blessing over us, and it was over.

Christyne never said a word about what she experienced that day, likely for fear of backlash. Then one day we talked about that morning at church.

"What did you feel? Weird?" I asked her.

"*Weird* is not the word I would use, Costi," she fired back so quickly I knew she was serious.

"Okay, describe it in your own words then," I said.

"It was the darkest feeling I have ever felt in my life. I was scared to death. Something pinned me down on the ground that felt like pure evil. My heart was racing and I have never felt so out of place in all my life."

Her words cut my heart open like a surgeon's knife.

"Are you serious?"

My question was rhetorical. We sat in silence for what seemed like hours, though it was only minutes. I will never forget that moment as years of questions, stories from other people, and even evidence from the Bible started to stack up. Maybe this was all from a very dark source.

One more attempt to get her fixed would push us over the edge.

3. *"She needs to speak in tongues."* It was another last-ditch effort to fix her in the summer of 2012. In anticipation of our wedding in October, Christyne had moved to Vancouver in June and was living in her own bedroom in our family home. A church from Oliver, British Columbia, called. They wanted me to speak at a youth conference and included an invitation to Christyne, asking that she share her testimony of how she became a Christian. I accepted on her behalf (something I don't recommend any man ever do), and after a few weeks of scolding me, she gave in. As an extreme introvert, she was upset about having to speak in front of a large crowd. *What's the big deal?* I thought. That was the last time I ever put her up to such a thing.

They provided her with separate sleeping arrangements, and we drove about five hours to Oliver.

The conference went well. During her session, Christyne taught with clarity and encouragement, and the teens loved her. Before we knew it, the conference was coming to a close and I was in the back room preparing to preach the final session.

The host pastor's wife, "Joan," approached me and said

loudly, "Costi, when you finish preaching, I want you to fill all the kids with the Holy Spirit and get them the gift of speaking in tongues. There are numerous kids we've been trying to reach in the community who are here and you've got their attention. Seal the deal!"

I nodded uncomfortably. *Oh, goodness. Here we go with the pressure to force tongues on teens.* I loathed the fact that I would have to try to get them to do something my own fiancee couldn't do.

I preached my guts out and closed in prayer. Joan glared at me and nodded as if to say, "Time to seal the deal." Feeling there was no choice, I went for it.

"If you want to be filled with the Holy Spirit, come down to the front of this platform. God is going to fill you today." My anxiety heightened and my mind was saying, *Don't do this,* but I had already gone too far. Then it hit me. *Time to call an audible. Joan isn't in control of this service. I am.*

One by one, I prayed for the kids in a generic way. I laid my hands on their shoulders, not their heads, and said, "Lord, fill them with your Spirit." That was it! I was going to pray that way, and if some kid got tongues, then so be it, but no way was I going to force something onto these kids that wasn't genuine.

My clever plan worked for a short time, then it blew up in my face. Joan came roaring up to the front, grabbed the mic out of my hand, and started shouting into it.

"Thank you, Brother Costi! Now kids, look at me! I want you to move your lips and just say what comes to the tip of your tongue. Sha-ba-ba-ba-ba-ba . . . Sha-ba-ba-ba-ba-ba . . . That's it! Just begin to call out anything you can. Ba-ta-ba-ba-ba-ta."

The coercing continued for more than ten minutes. Joan went around laying her hands on their heads and forcing them to say random syllables. Standing next to Christyne, I saw that she had her eyes closed and was trying to mumble syllables. My disgust at Joan's method soon faded, and I thought, *If this crazy lady can get Christyne to speak in tongues, then maybe I am the one who is crazy!*

The babbling continued another twenty minutes or so and then subsided. Joan congratulated all of the kids on their new spiritual gift, to use every day as a special prayer language, and told them they were now filled with the Spirit and sealed in the faith. Christyne and I said our goodbyes and got into the car for the five-hour drive home.

Within the first hundred kilometers (we were in Canada), I simmered with questions. I couldn't hold it in any longer.

"So," I broke the silence. "I saw you speaking in tongues, Christyne. You were doing it. I peeked at you while your eyes were closed during prayer. Did you get it?"

She tightened up her chin the way she does when she's about to cry. *Uh-oh.* I tried to think of something to say, but my mind was blank. Then the tears started to stream down her face.

"I tried, Costi. I really did. I lifted my hands like I was supposed to. I opened up my lips and said the syllables like she said to. I mumbled the words and did everything I was told. It didn't work. That was a complete show. She was manipulating kids into speaking in tongues. If it's a gift, wouldn't God be the one giving it? Why would someone have to coach a bunch of kids into doing something that only God can give them the ability to do?"

Hopeless and frustrated, we spent the remainder of the drive mostly in silence. I kept wondering why Christyne wasn't getting the Holy Spirit the way she was supposed to. We had been taught over and over that she needed to speak in tongues to prove she had the Holy Spirit and was saved. Was she not saved?

Soon after arriving home, we began to study the Bible together looking for answers. One day a verse jumped off the page. It was in a section of 1 Corinthians where the apostle Paul is explaining that different people have different gifts and that not everyone will have the same gifts—or even all the gifts—but that everybody uses what they've been given by God to do their part. In 1 Corinthians 12:29–30, Paul asks some rhetorical questions to make his point: "All are not apostles, are they? All are not prophets, are they? All are not teachers, are they? All are not workers of miracles, are they? All do not have gifts of healings, do they? All do not speak with tongues, do they? All do not interpret, do they?" His words hit us like a ton of bricks! We looked at each other, the same thought filling us with joy: *We're off the hook!*

Christyne asked, "Costi, does this mean what I think it does? It's plain as day! Not all people are going to operate in all the same gifts. I don't know everything about every verse in the Bible, but I know what that says. Not all speak in tongues!"

After all the pressure we'd been under to get Christyne to speak in tongues, relief flooded our hearts and minds. For the time being, our flawed belief system about speaking in tongues was debunked, and we grew evermore suspicious of other prosperity gospel beliefs. Soon, our view on healing would be put to the test as well.

4. *"She's not allowed to be sick."* The prosperity gospel teaches it is never God's will for his children to be sick, and sickness means you are the problem. Muster up enough faith or give a big enough offering, and you will get your healing. This belief often led to two things: (1) the bragging of prosperity gospel preachers from the pulpit that nobody in their house is sick, because they practice what they preach, and (2) prosperity gospel followers hiding their sickness for fear of being condemned in their community as someone with no faith.

Christyne's asthma was something we downplayed all the
time, because sickness was not allowed in the Hinn house. Until
one day when things took a very serious turn.

"Christyne?" I called down the basement stairwell of my parents' house.

Christyne had begun to spend much of her time down in the
basement to avoid my family. At this point in our journey together,
she wasn't getting tongues, she was not getting the Spirit, and she
was not falling at the feet of the family. With the wedding only
two months away, tensions were rising because the family was
trying to get her to conform, but nothing was working. Family
arguments ensued, comments were made, and the whole thing
turned ugly fast. Christyne was starting to break down.

I tried again. "Christyne?" But there was nothing but silence.

Her car was in the driveway; she wasn't in her room or anywhere in the house. *Maybe she's outside getting some air.* I wasn't sure
where she was, so I headed downstairs to be sure she wasn't there.

In the corner of the basement, a storage room door was open a
crack and I could see a body on the floor. Christyne! I rushed over
and tried to push the door all the way open, but it was blocked by
her body. I squeezed through the gap to find my bride-to-be paralyzed and gasping for air. I scanned her body, noticing her veins
were massive and bulging through her arms, wrists, and neck. I
took hold of her face and caught her fading eyes.

"Can you hear me?"

She nodded.

"What do I do with this?" I pointed at a little machine about
the size of an iPad that was next to her. It had a hose coming off
it and was turned on.

She motioned with her eyes as best as she could at a small

vial with fluid in it. I started asking more questions, telling her to blink if the answer was yes. She was barely breathing when I got the fluid into the tube and it created a vapor she could breathe in. I shoved the tube into her mouth. Her hands were withered and crippled.

As I held on to one of her hands, a tear started to slowly run down her face.

"Do I need to call an ambulance?" I asked. She shook her head no.

Within several minutes, her body was released from paralysis and she could talk. She explained that she had just had a severe asthma attack. I was certain it was stress related, because this had never happened since I knew her.

"Why are you in the basement storage room with this machine? Shouldn't this be right next to your bed or in your closet where you can get to it at all times?" I asked.

"I've been hiding it," she explained. "I know we can't talk about my asthma because sickness is not allowed in your home. I put my medicine and nebulizer in this storage room so your parents won't find it if they ever go through my stuff."

Her response to this question was all I needed to hear. My blood was boiling. Enough was enough. I didn't know what I was going to do, but I knew it was time to get her out of this environment.

Mum Has a Tumor

During 2011 and 2012, while Christyne was being put through the pressures of the Hinn family fix, my mother received the news that a tumor had formed on the front part of her brain.

"A tumor? Are you sure?"

The words didn't seem real as they slipped off my tongue. My dad, understandably uncomfortable, quickly chimed in, "She's going to be fine. God will heal her. He probably already has."

This was uncharted territory for our side of the Hinn family. It was my mom, and she had a tumor. For several months, it had caused all sorts of problems for her, but we had no idea. Doctors had misdiagnosed her several times, no prophetic words of knowledge were working, and finally, they found the issue. *How in the world is this possible?* I thought. The Hinn family never got sick. Or at least we never admitted it when we were.

Sickness that was supposed to stay so far from our home had infiltrated the heartbeat of our home—my mum. Christyne's circumstances could be chalked up to her being an outsider who didn't have the special anointing we had. But when the matriarch of our family was hit with a tumor, all bets were off.

It took nearly four years for my mother to be properly diagnosed because of a mixture of denial, avoidance, lack of support from my father, and the time it takes for doctors to properly diagnose these things. During that time, my father downplayed her sickness. He preached that we are all to be healthy and whole while my own mother sat silently in the front row with a tumor waging war on her brain. Doctor's visits were done when my father was out of town. My mother hid the negative reports, and if she even hinted at the word tumor, my father would rebuke her and the word tumor in the name of Jesus. Finally, however, all the prosperity gospel power in the world could do nothing. With no choice but to pursue medical intervention, they faced the facts. It would be a surgeon's hand that healed my mother.

I'll never forget going to the hospital in Vancouver to visit

Mum during her recovery. My stomach was in knots. It was so foreign for our family to be in a hospital. We were barely allowed in hospitals growing up because we were told that the spirit of infirmity and the spirit of death lived there. Now here we were, and it was the ultimate shock to the prosperity gospel system. No amount of prayer or faith had done the healing. Not one of the healers in our family just showed up to handle it. The experience put a serious hole in the prosperity gospel foundation I'd come to depend on in the face of adversity. When we needed healing the most, it wasn't divine healing that solved the issue. It was medication and the skilled hands of a human surgeon.

My mother's tumor became another layer on the mountain of evidence building against the prosperity gospel. *God is a healer. But something about the way we teach that and the way we live that doesn't add up.*

I wondered about it all, but I still had no real answers.

California, Here We Come . . . Again

All that summer of 2012, I prayed for direction. Day after day for weeks on end, I asked God for a way out of the life we were stuck living. With no money but the money I made through my family, no real job skills, and no opportunities for escape, we were stuck in Vancouver. The church was going well as far as growth and relationships went—the people loved Christyne and treated her well. But my family was crushing her day after day. Soon, I was blaming her as well and wondering why she couldn't just fake some things to keep the peace. It was all very toxic. With the wedding in October, I was crying out to God for help because I didn't think we'd make it. On multiple occasions, I had suicidal thoughts because I felt so trapped in the world we had bought in to. On the outside, it was mansions, money, and big promises. On the inside, it was verbal and spiritual abuse, deception, and torment.

Then, out of nowhere, came an answer to prayer.

I received a text message from my friend, Brett. Brett was the community pastor at the church plant we had left before moving to Canada—and a huge hockey fan like me. He asked to skype. When we got on the video call, he was a sight for sore eyes! His big smile and red beard were a welcome interruption to the pain Christyne and I were experiencing.

"Hey, man!" he said with his usual enthusiasm. "How are things going over there, you big world changer!" We used that term a lot to describe what we wanted to do. We wanted to change the world. But I definitely wasn't.

I had told him when I left that I was going to revitalize my dad's church and change the world in Vancouver. I loved the city and the people where I grew up. Brett, a big fan of reaching people, cheered us on all the way.

Unfortunately, all that world change was just a pipe dream. I had to come clean.

"It's terrible, man," I confessed. "The church is doing okay, but everything else is terrible. Christyne isn't getting whatever special anointing my family thinks she should. They are constantly mistreating her. Now she is pulling back from them. I'm starting to go head-to-head with my dad to defend Christyne. It's turned into a war in this house, and I have no idea what to do."

Brett didn't flinch. It was as though God had ordained the Skype call and Brett was the perfect man for the job.

"Well, this might hit a nerve, so don't punch me when you see me, okay?" He laughed, but I knew he was serious.

"Okay, I won't hit you. What is it?"

"Sounds like you need to stop trying to be your dad's hero by saving his church, and start being Christyne's hero because she's your future wife." Then he said four words that seared my heart like a branding iron.

"She's your first ministry."

I went silent as a volcano of truth erupted, destroying my misconceptions about marriage and ministry. I was always taught that ministry was number one. My uncle had lost his own marriage because he was married to ministry. We had married friends from TBN who acted happily married on TV to keep donor money coming in, but they lived in separate houses in the same neighborhood. Marriage was just for show. Ministry was everything! I had watched our own family be put on the back burner all the time for ministry. Money had to be made and ministry had to be done. The family was an afterthought. Now Brett was telling me that Christyne was my first ministry and that she was my number one priority? *How does that work?* I thought.

Swallowing my pride, I knew I had no choice. "I need help," I pleaded.

"I know you do," he assured me. "Here's what you're going to do. First, you're going to pray about coming here to California, because we have a job for you. We're still trying to get this church plant established and need a part-time youth pastor. It's not glamorous and we've only got nine kids, but we're just getting started. You'll need another part-time job, and Christyne will need to find a job too, but where God guides, God provides.

"Also," he continued, "you're going to take Christyne out on a date and tell her she's your first ministry and you'll love and protect her because God designed it that way. Then, you tell her you're leaving Vancouver. Pick a few states where you think you might have opportunities for work and let her speak into it. If it's not California, that's fine—I'll be praying for you. All that matters is that you put her above yourself. Vancouver is not a healthy scenario for you two. No matter how much you love your parents or their church, she needs to know you'd give that up for her."

A deep breath later, I agreed. A date night later, Christyne agreed.

California, here we come. Again.

8

Transformed by the Truth

One of the cruelest lies of contemporary "faith healers" is that the people they fail to heal are guilty of sinful unbelief, a lack of faith, or "negative confession."

—JOHN F. MACARTHUR

"Hi, Costi! Good to talk to you." The familiar face on the Skype call warmly greeted me.

"Hi, Pastor Tony! Thanks for taking the time to talk today."

I was on another video call with the church in California. This time, it was the teaching pastor, Anthony Wood (though his friends call him Tony). I was a bit more nervous than in previous conversations because he was interviewing me for the final time before hiring me. After a series of questions, he got to the point.

"So, Costi, is a nine-kid youth ministry too small time for a guy like you, or do you like pioneering new ministries?"

"A nine-kid youth ministry sounds awesome! Pioneering new ministries does too. I'm just thankful for the opportunity to come out there and serve!" I was jubilant. This was the rescue I needed, so I wasn't about to blow it. I would do anything if it meant being in a place where people wanted truth.

"Okay. What about your doctrinal positions? For example, what's your view on the book of Revelation?" he quizzed.

I started to stammer. "Um, well, I . . . I'm not sure, but I can figure that out if you need me to." My face must have been going red because he eased up.

"Hey, hey, it's okay, buddy, relax. We'll get all that sorted out soon enough. I can help." He reassured me they were excited to have me out there and that he'd see me soon. Neither one of us knew there was a bigger storyline happening at the time. He just needed a guy to help with the youth. I needed a church to help me escape the world I was in and point me to the truth.

Leaving the Prosperity Gospel Lifestyle Behind

That first week in California flew by. Right off the bat, we got married, which was a whirlwind of God's grace! Not only did a beautiful church with an ocean view do us a huge favor by letting us use their facility, but Christyne's parents put as much money toward the wedding as they could. Truth be told, a lot of things were booked with the "Hinn lifestyle" in mind long before the transition took place. This meant an Orange County wedding near the finest hotels with the amenities to appease their preferences.

On Sunday of our wedding week, we were introduced to the church plant we'd be serving, called Moment Church. (Eventually we changed the name to Mission Bible Church.) In the midst of all the joy, there was backlash against us for leaving the Hinn family circle. By the time we crossed the border, Christyne was officially charged with "ruining the anointing on my life," but we didn't care and had not an ounce of bitterness in our hearts. We were newlyweds with a new start. No more spiritual abuse. No more confusion. No more lies. We had transitioned from California to Canada and back to California in just two years. Little did we know that God was setting us up for the biggest transition yet. But first, God would strip everything away and test our hearts in ways we'd never imagined.

Although we were free from the prosperity gospel abuses, we were now subject to making it on our own. By God's grace, the church was able to pay me several hundred dollars per month, but I still needed to find a job to make ends meet. I landed one and started making ten dollars per hour doing contract work for an athletic company. Hardly enough to make ends meet, but it was a start. Christyne landed a job as well, but we had to live sixty miles away from Orange County in order to survive.

During our first four months in California, we lived in a foreclosing house that someone let us use. The bank was taking it over within months but said we were welcome to stay in it rent free until then. Any romantic newlywed dreams we may have had of lying in bed all day together and staring into each other's eyes were quickly shattered by the fact that we had to drive 120 miles round trip six days per week just to afford food, our bills, and to save up to be able to pay rent in an apartment. We slept on an old mattress on the floor surrounded by our

clothes, which hung on racks. Our room was scarcely naviga-
ble because our belongings were piled everywhere. The upstairs
was occupied by roommates who were also using the free ride
to survive for a few months. It was utter chaos.

But just like my friend Brett had told me, "Where God guides,
God provides." And God did. A few months later, we had put away
enough money to pay our deposit on an apartment, and after getting some old furniture from friends, we started selling some of
our prosperity gospel treasures to pay off the wedding debt my
family left us. I sold watches, other jewelry, and valuables. I had
already downsized from a Hummer to a cheap Chrysler, then had
to do away with that as well because I couldn't afford the payment. We began to share a car. Oh, "first world problems!" But it
was a big change for me.

Next thing we knew, we were living two miles from church,
and though it was no prosperity gospel lifestyle, it was our life. I
had gone from living in nearly ten thousand square feet to living
in six hundred square feet. From driving a Hummer, to driving
a Chrysler, to driving a Kia Soul, to riding my bike because my
wife needed the car to go to work. From shopping Versace to
scouring Marshalls. From five-star restaurants to date night at
Del Taco, when we could afford the dollar tacos. It wasn't glamorous, but it was honest. There were no luxuries, but there was
no guilt either. People may have thought we had failed, but we
felt we had hit the jackpot. I had peace. I could sleep at night. No
one was being exploited because of my decisions. Even though
those early months were the hardest we had ever faced, it felt
like this was the right track to be on, the right way to start out
in ministry.

Firm on Truth, Flexible with People

During the first few months at the church, nobody really noticed I was a Hinn. A few people knew, but they didn't make a big deal about it. I was treated like anybody else and formed relationships based on who I was, not on what my last name was. Brett and I continued to enjoy friendship, and soon, Pastor Tony and I were going out for lunch and having interesting discussions.

At thirty-four, Tony was a fun pastor, but he'd started to become very serious when it came to the truth. But while he was dogmatic about certain truths, he was patient and flexible with those who were stuck in ignorance. That's how he approached conversations with me about prosperity preaching, faith healing, and my family background. On the way back from a lunch meeting one day, he asked a loaded question.

"So what do you think of all that healing stuff your family teaches?"

"I'm not all that sure," I replied. "I know God heals, but so many things they teach don't seem to add up. We always attached money to healing, so it was a lot like the prosperity gospel and healing all together. I love my family, but so much didn't add up." I responded as broadly as possible because I didn't want to say anything stupid.

His tone changed. "Yeah, well, I'm not sold on that stuff either. It's a dangerous way to go." *What does he know that I don't?* But at that point, I wasn't ready to ask.

As I watched Pastor Tony's life in the months that followed, I saw a man who was honest about his humanity and shortcomings, but ferociously devoted to truth. He never claimed to be perfect, but he was always progressing as a leader. It was a balance of grace and guts I had never seen before. He loved people but refused to compromise. He would tell you the hardest truth you'd ever been told, but his eyes would tear up as he did. It was pastoral ministry in a way no one in my world ever pastored.

Not only was Pastor Tony different from what I was used to, but the whole ministry was a revelation. No one on the staff lived lavishly while everyone else suffered. The church budgeted responsibly and made sure people had a solid living wage. The congregation and church leaders were accountable to each other. And craziest of all, Pastor Tony deliberately talked about money only once per year in January! He would teach a series on what the Bible says about money, then we'd all commit to generously support the church and serve our community with our resources, and that was it! We didn't really talk about money, and the church was healthy and generous with its resources.

Talk about culture shock. It all seemed so counterintuitive. *Is this the version of church I've been looking for? The leadership is different. The teaching is different. The people are different. I think this is how church is supposed to be.*

A Life-Changing Passage

Pastor Tony walked into my office one afternoon and said, "I need you to preach while I am away."

I grinned from ear to ear, quickly thanked him, and told him I was excited at the opportunity. We were in a series on the Gospel of John, going through it verse by verse. He'd been coaching me through various Bible study methods and helping our staff go deeper in their faith and doctrine. So when he handed me a commentary, it was nothing surprising—except for the thickness of it. Clunk! The book hit my desk as he said, "This is a good commentary. It should help keep the train on the tracks." He was referring to the trusted commentary being a useful tool to keep pastors from preaching something that was outside of biblical bounds, the sort of thing a kid from a prosperity gospel background might do after years of living out false beliefs.

"Your preaching assignment is John 5:1–17. That's where we are in the Gospel of John series, so just pick it up from there and keep us going," he explained. "I'll need your preliminary notes by next week. We'll meet and go over them. I'll offer some suggestions and critiques, then you'll revise them and send me your final notes the Friday before you preach. Got it?"

"Yes, sir!" I was exuberant.

Eager to start studying, I blocked time off on my calendar and got right to work. I took my Bible and opened it to the passage. The header in my Bible said, "The Healing at Bethesda." I knew the story well. Jesus healed a man who had been sick for a long time. A sermon on healing, just what I specialized in.

As I began to study, I used the strategies I had been learning for the last five months at the church. First, I read the text over and over and wrote down observations and questions each time I read it. I still have my sermon notes. Here are some of those observations and questions:

4.30.2013, Preliminary Notes & Observations, John 5:1–17

John 5:3—" . . . *a multitude* of those who were sick, blind, lame, and withered . . .": Jesus saw a multitude of sick people but only healed one man in this story. Why didn't he heal them all?

What was so special about this man? Did he have more faith than others? Was he a friend of Jesus?

John 5:6–7—When Jesus asked the man, *"Do you wish to get well?"* The man answered with a sort of complaint and a sob story. He didn't say, "YES! JESUS, HEAL ME!" Or, "I HAVE FAITH TO BE HEALED!"

John 5:8–9—"Jesus said to him, '**Arise**, take up your pallet, and walk.' And **immediately** the man **became well**, and **took up his pallet** and **began to walk**." This shows Jesus' creative power. The healing was immediate! No process. No music. No special service. No offering. No fanfare. He healed the sick man with a word. Arise!

John 5:12–13—"They asked him, 'Who is the man who said to you, "Take up your pallet, and walk"?' But he who was healed **did not know** who it was; for Jesus had slipped away while there was a crowd in that place." The Greek word for "know" that is used here is *eido*. This word means "to know, to perceive, be aware of." That means that the man didn't even know who Jesus was. How could he have faith to be healed if he didn't even know who Jesus was? How could he even believe in Jesus if he didn't know Jesus? Was faith involved at all? How could faith be involved if he was passive in receiving his healing and ignorant of who the Healer was? Was any money involved? There is no indication of this man doing anything for Jesus to get a healing. Jesus seems to have healed the man out of his own volition and desire to do so.

Each one of these observations put a devastating crack in the foundation of my theology within the first couple of hours of study. I couldn't believe what I was reading, but at the same time, it was all starting to become clear, like a camera slowly shifting focus from blurry to high-definition resolution.

First of all, Jesus healed one man out of a multitude of sick people. I always believed and was taught that everybody was always supposed to get healed. Prosperity theology teaches that it's always God's will to heal everybody, and that if they are sick, it's their own fault because they don't have enough faith or haven't given a special offering to get healed.

Healings in my world were also said to be a process sometimes. That way we could take their money and say something like, "Keep on believing in faith that God will do it in a day or so." But Jesus healed this man immediately. We always had hours of music, special healing lines, healing products like oil, and special commands given to people in order to get their healing. It was as though we were offering a menu for people to get their healing, but Jesus just went in and healed without a problem. He most certainly didn't have catchers, nor did he knock people over repeatedly or tell the man to give him a seed-faith offering to receive his healing.

My heart was racing. I needed to know more and do some digging, so I reached for the commentary Pastor Tony had given me. I opened the commentary and began to read John MacArthur's notes on the passage:

> Unlike many alleged modern healings, Jesus' healings were complete and instantaneous, with or without faith. This one proves the point, since the man exhibited no faith in Jesus at all. Yet he was healed instantly and wholly. John records that "immediately . . . he became well, and picked up his pallet and began to walk." One of the cruelest lies of contemporary

"faith healers" is that the people they fail to heal are guilty of sinful unbelief, a lack of faith, or a "negative confession." In contrast, those whom Jesus healed did not always manifest faith beforehand (cf. Matt. 8:14–15; 9:32–33; 12:10–13, 22; Mark 7:32–35; 8:22–25; Luke 14:1–4; 22:50–51; John 9:1–7), and this man is a prime example. This incident perfectly illustrates God's sovereign grace in action (cf. v. 21). Out of all the sick people at the pool, Jesus chose to heal this man. There was nothing about him that made him more deserving than the others, nor did he seek out Jesus; Jesus approached him. The Lord did not choose him because He foresaw that he had the faith to believe for a healing; he never did express belief that Jesus could heal him. So it is in salvation. Out of the spiritually dead multitude of Adam's fallen race, God chose and redeemed His elect—not because of anything they did to deserve it, or because of their foreseen faith, but because of His sovereign choice (6:37; Rom. 8:29–30; 9:16; Eph. 1:4–5; 2:4–5; 2 Thess. 2:13; Titus 3:5). Even the faith to believe was a sovereign gift (Eph. 2:8–9).[1]

I had traveled the world, seen all there was to see, and lived like royalty, but this moment outshone the brightest diamonds we'd ever owned. The words seemed to leap off the page, and the once-blurry picture of who God is and what the gospel is suddenly came into sharp focus.

Coach Heefner's words from my Dallas Baptist baseball days came back to me: God is sovereign. This is what he meant all

---

1   John MacArthur, *The MacArthur New Testament Commentary: John 1–11* (Chicago: Moody, 2006), 175.

along. God is in control. He's not some cosmic genie who exists to give me what I want and do what I command him to do. He is the majestic Creator of heaven and earth whom we exist to worship. He heals at will because of his power. He saves our lost souls because of his mercy. He calls us to a purpose greater than ourselves, and we owe him our lives. He can't be controlled with an offering. He doesn't heal if we just have enough faith. And he most certainly does not require money, special music, and a mystical healing televangelist to accomplish his divine purpose.

The gospel suddenly made sense. My life existed for the glory of God, not my own glory. God's highest purpose was not to make me happy, healthy, and wealthy; it was to give him glory!

On April 30, 2013, right there in the middle of my sermon preparation, I had what Pastor Tony calls my "grace awakening" moment. I began to cry about things I had never cried about before. I saw in my mind the faces of so many hurting people and was broken to pieces over the role I had played in exploiting them with false hope. For so long, I had wanted answers but couldn't find them. Now I could finally see the full truth. Over the course of what seemed to be hours, I repented of my sins, false teachings, and life of hypocrisy. I confessed to God that I had twisted his gospel for greedy gain, and I asked him to forgive me and give me a fresh start. I committed to studying the truth, preaching the truth, and standing up for the truth no matter what the cost. The real Jesus was now my Lord, and the real gospel was now my life. I was ready to do whatever it took to make things right, and I promised him I would do whatever the church needed me to do as well.

It didn't take long before I'd have to.

From a Heavenly High to a Humbling Low

It wasn't long before I found myself in Pastor Tony's office telling him what I had experienced and, of course, what I was going to do.

"It was a lie! We twisted Scripture! We manipulated people! We smeared the gospel!" I was in high gear without any sign of slowing down. "I have to do something about this! Innocent people are being hurt. Worst of all, Jesus is being misrepresented. I know things no one does, and everything makes sense now. I've got to do something about this!"

As I went from one exclamatory statement to the next, Pastor Tony sat back in his chair as cool and collected as ever, just smiling and nodding away. Having been in ministry for a lot longer than me, and being the son and grandson of pastors, he had seen this a thousand times. We have a term around the office for this sort of thing. It's humorously called "cage stage." Cage stage means that when you come to realize some big-time truth for the first time and your emotions get the best of you, you're better off being put in a cage for a little while to keep you under control so you don't do or say something stupid. Did I ever need to be caged!

He began to talk me down off the ledge. "No, you're not going to do something. At least not yet. Jesus has a good handle on his gospel, and you're not the first to realize these truths."

His words deflated my bubble of zeal.

"I have a question for you, Costi." He paused long enough for me to catch my breath and prepare for what was about to come next.

"Do you want to be a pastor?"

"Of course I do. It's what I am called to be. I can't imagine doing anything else with my life." I felt like a son pleading with his father for his dreams and desires but knowing he needed direction.

"Then be a pastor and do what a pastor does." His words were so definitive it was impossible to misunderstand. "Serve the church, be faithful, study hard, and if God decides to open a door for you to do something about this evil, then go for it. But don't assume this world needs you any more than it needs me or anyone else. God is in control. He is sovereign over everything, and he decides who he is going to use in ministry and how far that ministry is going to go. You focus on faithfulness. God will decide the rest."

I knew exactly what he meant, but it was a tough pill to swallow. No matter how much I wanted to confront the evils of the prosperity gospel, my efforts would prove futile if I wasn't faithful in what God had put in front of me. I needed to keep my mouth shut, do my job, serve the church, and rebuild my theology based on a proper interpretation of Scripture. Even though I was aware of the deception I had been a part of, I needed to grow in the truth.

Facing the Cold, Hard Facts

It was a breezy spring evening in Southern California. I cracked open a window and closed the door to our bedroom. John MacArthur, the author of the commentary I had used for my sermon, also has a ministry called Grace to You, which provides excellent Bible resources on any topic you can think of. A friend from Grace to You had sent me one of their DVDs titled *A Deeper Healing* and recommended I give it my undivided attention. He said this DVD teaching series would help me face more of the facts about healing and the false hope that teachers like my uncle proliferated.

I loaded the disc and hit play. A woman in a wheelchair appeared. *Oh,* I thought. *This looks interesting.*

Her story quickly captured my attention. It picked up steam, and soon I was hanging on her every word. There she sat in a wheelchair, sharing her testimony in front of a large crowd, and it was going very differently than I had been used to. There was no healer. There were no catchers. And it seemed there was no grand miracle. Only pain. Soon, my heart began to pound as she questioned where God was in her quadriplegia. Unhealed by a famous faith healer in her day, she cried out to God in confusion.

"What kind of Savior, what kind of Rescuer, what kind of Healer, what kind of Deliverer would refuse the prayer of a paralytic?" she exclaimed. Lost in her frustration and set on shutting the world out, Joni Eareckson Tada set her feet in the concrete of bitterness. No healing? Fine. No joy!

But there in the darkness of her pain, the light of truth crept through the cracks of her heart and out of her mouth came a song. She began to sing right there in the middle of her message:

> Abide with me, fast falls the eventide
> When darkness deepens, Lord, with me abide
> When other helpers fail and comforts flee
> Help of the helpless, oh, abide with me

And abide with her the Master did. Soon she turned to the Scriptures for wisdom and found the truth she needed to take each day as it came.

I could not believe what I was seeing and hearing. Then again, I had never heard of Joni Eareckson Tada until that moment either. Inspired by her circumstances and incredible commitment to God's Word, I was again pushed to look to God's Word for answers. It was in that moment, through tears, watching a paralyzed woman share truths in a way I had never heard before, that I began to fully understand what Jesus came to do and who he came to be. Yes, he was a healer, but he was so much more than that.

That message by Joni was one of many dominoes God used to help me learn the truth. Over the course of that next year, everything in my life changed. Here's the short list:

- I got biblically baptized after what I considered to be my true conversion.
- I was stripped of my title of pastor and became a pastor in training.
- Family members cut me off after I tried to privately reach them with truth.
- The Lord opened doors for further mentorship from faithful pastors.
- Our church enhanced its policies for hiring staff members and training leaders.
- I sought biblical counseling to learn from the past and prepare for the future.
- Pastor Tony gave me more than a hundred books from his family's pastoral collection so I could study sound doctrine.
- I started seminary.

It was a year to remember.

New Heroes in the Faith

As my theological understanding changed, so did my heroes in
the faith. I turned to the Bible and studied the trustworthy leaders who stood tall in the New Testament. Peter and the disciples
left everything to follow Jesus (Matt. 19:27), and Stephen was
martyred for his bold preaching of the truth (Acts 7:54–60).
Jude contended for the faith no matter the cost (Jude 3). Paul was
beaten and imprisoned for the sake of the gospel and was never
one to mince words when it came to false teachers (Gal. 1:8–9). As
my study deepened, it became painfully clear that the Hinn style
of ministry was nothing like the real gospel ministry described in
Scripture. We resembled the greedy magicians and imposters that
the Bible repeatedly calls out (Acts 8:9–21; 2 Peter 2:1–3). It was
one truth-punch to the gut after another, but I'd never felt better.

Beyond biblical history, church history painted a grim picture
of the type of people who preached poisonous doctrines in the
church and abused power to get rich. The Reformation changed
the course of the church forever when men grew tired of the
exploitation of the poor and the selling of papal indulgences by the
Catholic Church, along with heretical teaching that was polluting
faith and worship. Martin Luther stood against the false teachings
of the Catholic Church, and many others paid a heavy price for
being faithful. There was no arguing with history. God had never
taken kindly to prosperity gospel pundits or power hungry abusers. He cleaned house every time! Faithfulness was not getting rich
by teaching people to give you all their money. Faithfulness was
glorifying God, obeying him, and loving him above all and your
neighbor as yourself. Faithfulness for a pastor meant giving your
life to serve the church, not having the church serve you.

Soon, I found inspiration in the heroism of William Tyndale, who was strangled, then burned at the stake by the king of England, but not before providing the world with the best English Bible translation it had ever had. Even at the stake, his final words were said to be, "Lord! Open the king of England's eyes." That kind of passion for truth paired with a passion for lives to be changed stirred my soul in a way I had never experienced before.

Missionaries like Hudson Taylor, who spent more than fifty years serving China for the sake of the gospel, were nothing like the prosperity gospel heroes I once revered. Charles Spurgeon preached his guts out in the nineteenth century and was a staunch defender of the faith. He became incredibly famous but never once used the gospel as a means to a life of luxurious ease. Instead, he used his notoriety to put the gospel front and center and channeled his storehouse of resources into gospel advancement projects. Another giant in the faith, J. C. Ryle, cautioned churches long ago about the likes of Benny Hinn and those whose false doctrines were subtly camouflaged by layers of truth: "Now this 'subtlety,' St. Paul tells us, is precisely what we have to fear in false doctrine. We are not to expect it to approach our minds in the garment of error, but in the form of truth. Bad coin would never obtain currency if it had not some likeness to good. The wolf would seldom get into the fold if he did not enter it in sheep's clothing. . . . Satan is far too wise a general to manage a campaign in such a fashion as this."[2]

Modern-day theologians and legends of the Christian faith—both still alive and recently passed—also played a critical role in my growth and understanding. John MacArthur, Warren Wiersbe,

---

2 J. C. Ryle, *Warnings to the Churches* (Edinburgh: Banner of Truth, 2016), 131.

R. C. Sproul, Martyn Lloyd-Jones, Millard Erickson, W. A. Criswell, Norman Geisler, John Walvoord, F. F. Bruce, and numerous other faithful teachers line my bookshelves, their works pointing to Scripture on nearly every topic a Christian would need for a doctrinal overhaul. Beyond that, I enrolled in seminary and started studying biblical Greek at Talbot School of Theology before transferring to Midwestern Baptist Theological Seminary.

The facts were the facts. Everything that biblical history, church history, and modern-day faithful preachers described about false teachers and greedy church abusers fit our profile to a tee. Though many of my heroes were dead preachers, I suddenly felt like I had found long-lost family members and friends in the faith I wished I could meet. Their example of humility, faithfulness, and fierce devotion to the truth was enough to push me into action. Most of all, the Jesus Christ of the Scriptures was my Savior and Lord. That was all the motivation I needed to move forward. I wanted to be a real pastor, shepherding the flock in faithfulness and not for selfish gain. I wanted to be a bold servant of Christ, the kind who preached the truth and called out error no matter the cost to protect people for the glory of God.

9

A Dangerously Abusive Theology

False doctrine has been the chosen engine which Satan has employed in every age to stop the progress of the gospel of Christ.

—J. C. RYLE

After an article about my conversion story was featured in *Christianity Today* in the fall of 2017, I received emails, tweets, and Facebook messages from people all over the world. These people explained how their lives had been devastated as a result of my uncle's life and ministry. Many were stories of hope because these people had been rescued from deception as well, but many had undergone such brutal abuse that my blood boiled as I read their words of pain. Their emotional state after all they'd been through closely mirrored someone who suffers from post-traumatic stress disorder (PTSD).

One man, whom I remembered well from my days working with my uncle, wrote me to ask for prayer. He traveled to many healing crusades and was an avid believer in my uncle. He explained that his wife and he were unable to have a baby but were told to sow a seed of faith into my uncle's ministry and God would give them a baby. They gave a financial gift—nothing happened. They did this again and again, finally taking all they had from savings and giving it as an offering, hoping God would give them a baby—their ultimate request—if they made the ultimate financial sacrifice.

My heart shattered as I read the message, knowing that in the end this couple was broke and my uncle was bankrolling their savings. Thankfully, that man and his wife quit following the prosperity gospel and found true faith in the midst of their suffering, but the damage done by the abusive teaching left scars they will never forget.

Elly Achok Olare is a pastor in Kenya who was once a prosperity gospel and Word of Faith preacher. (Word of Faith is the name for a theology that teaches you can obtain material wealth and healing by "speaking it into existence." It twists the kind of confession we see in the Bible concerning sin, and says that confession not only saves but can give you the power to obtain anything you want.) His story of God saving him out of the life he and his wife were leading is enough to break your heart. About the events leading up to his conversion, Olare writes about one of the most heartwrenching experiences:

> In 2003 my wife and I lost our first child, Whitney. I believed
> the "spirit of death" had prevailed over me. Turmoil ensued

for me and my equally Word of Faith-filled wife. How could God let the Devil overrun us like this?

Well-meaning church people suggested our calamity could be due to sin in our lives, or to a curse, or, as I firmly believed, to a lack of faith. My grieving wife and I spent months repenting of possible hidden sin. We also sought answers from our families in case of a generational curse—a dominant teaching in the Word of Faith movement.

During this time of inner turmoil, my wife became pregnant again. And on the sunny afternoon we took home our newborn son, Robin, we were jubilant in the triumph of a healthy baby. But the next twenty-four hours became the darkest time of our lives.

When Robin developed complications, we went into frenzied spiritual warfare along with a wide net of friends who interceded to God on our behalf. This time we would not be caught off guard. Our faith assured us the Devil would not take Robin. We called on those who gave us "prophetic" assurances: only life was permitted; death was not our portion. But the night grew more intense.

At the time, my wife believed she had a prophetic gift. Her visions that night included Robin playing happily in the mud, and a grown-up Robin addressing thousands as an international preacher. In tears she shared these images with me in the presence of prayer warriors gathered in our small house.

After midnight, when Robin's condition grew worse, a new prophetic word explained the Word of Faith error by indicating his healing had now been placed in the hands of a doctor. I left home clutching my baby and seeking the hospital.

At 3:00 a.m., the doctor looked into my determined eyes to declare the worst news I could hear. Robin was dead.

I carried my son's dead body back home to my wife. Though exhausted, she looked up and called me "Daddy," an endearment she'd never used. "He is all right now," she continued. "Bring him to me; I want to feed him."

I screamed from the deepest recesses of my being that dark morning as my wife and I fought over Robin's body. We had believed in our power over death itself. Prayer for our son's resurrection from the dead became a circus that only served to fortify our pain.

As my world collapsed, chaotic feelings assailed me. At one point I screamed at God in disappointment that he'd failed me again. I had exercised tremendous faith; how could God let this happen?

Next came a series of early miscarriages. Without answers, we were dismayed with God, whose ways no longer made sense to us. Though faith became a mirage, we kept up appearances, trying to pretend we didn't despair. Yet inwardly we felt doubtful, hopeless, even cursed.

How could we reconcile these bad things with a good God? Our Word of Faith teaching instructed us to dismiss Job's suffering as a consequence of his negative confession: "The Lord gave, and the Lord has taken away" (Job 1:21). But how could we make sense of Paul himself falling sick (Gal. 4:13) and yet rejoicing in his afflictions (2 Cor. 12:10)? How could we continue to reconcile this portrait with modern "super-apostles" who market health and wealth in their books, DVDs, and mega-meetings?

In my faith crisis and anger at God, I vowed to quit the

ministry. I felt like a fraud for preaching a "gospel" that did not work. God had become an enigma, and faith a labyrinth.[1]

These are just a few of countless stories I keep on file as a constant reminder that we have a responsibility to speak for those who have had their voices and dignity stripped from them, or who have had their deepest faith in God shaken or even destroyed. Most of all, we have a responsibility to stand for Jesus Christ when his name is dragged through the mud by charlatans.

Space does not allow me to cover as much teaching as I'd like to, and this chapter will barely scratch the surface of the prosperity gospel's abuses. That being said, it should be enough to help every reader gain an introductory understanding to the origin and spread of the prosperity gospel, as well as what the Bible has to say about this dangerous false teaching.

Where Did the Prosperity Gospel Come From?

The prosperity gospel finds its theological roots in what is called New Thought, which is essentially a metaphysical healing cult founded on the idea that the mind is the key to unlocking your true reality. This movement goes back to the 1800s, and while several people played significant roles in its proliferation, Phineas Quimby (1802–1866) is arguably the most influential. The father of New Thought, he was an American philosopher, hypnotist, and spiritualist. He did not claim to be aligned with classic

---

1   Patti Richter, Elly Achok Olare, *The Gospel Coalition*, "How God Saved Me from the Prosperity Gospel," August 17, 2016, www.thegospelcoalition.org/article/how-god-saved-me-from -the-prosperity-gospel/.

Christianity or the orthodox teachings of the Bible, but his philosophies invaded Christian theology. Quimby's beliefs that are
relevant to this subject can be summarized as follows:

- All sickness and disease originates in the mind.
- Healing can be obtained with right thinking.
- Quimby believed he had discovered the secret healing
  methods of Jesus.
- Jesus was an ordinary man using mind-control methods
  to heal.
- Quimby denied the bodily resurrection of Jesus.
- Hypnotism is the key to healing.

Although Quimby was not a Christian or a pastor, his philosophies have spread through Christianity like wildfire. That is
mainly because of the pastors who borrowed Quimby's ideologies
to spice up their ministry material, starting with Norman Vincent
Peale (1898–1993), pastor of Marble Collegiate Church in New
York City. Peale published a book in the 1950s called *The Power of
Positive Thinking*, which helped New Thought beliefs spread even
farther. American Christianity was witnessing the Trojan horse
rolling right through the city gates.

Next came men like E. W. Kenyon (1867–1948), who was
not explicitly New Thought in his theology, but its ideology is
found in his teachings. Kenyon is the most influential teacher
in the life of the infamous Kenneth E. Hagin (1917–2003), who
became a Word of Faith theology icon and controversial preacher.
Hagin in turn became the spiritual father to self-proclaimed billionaire preacher Kenneth Copeland (1936–). During the same
time, Oral Roberts (1918–2009) steadily headlined the explosion

of televangelism and rock-star prosperity preachers who claimed to heal the sick and rain down blessings from Jesus. These men became the household names for "name it and claim it" theology and the prosperity gospel. Today, they are revered as heroes in the faith by my uncle Benny, Joel Osteen (whose father, John Osteen, loved Kenneth Hagin), Joyce Meyer, Maurice Cerullo, and many others.

How Did the Prosperity Gospel Get So Popular?

This still doesn't quite answer the big question: how in the world did this scam posing as Christianity get so popular? It's one thing to know where it came from. But seeing how it came to fool so many people is equally as important.

The prosperity gospel appeals to the deep longing of every human heart for peace, health, wealth, and happiness. There is nothing wrong with wanting a good and happy life, but the prosperity gospel uses Jesus Christ as a pawn in its get-rich-quick scam. The prosperity gospel sells salvation and false hope. But true and lasting peace can be found only through faith in the Lord, Jesus Christ. More on that in the next chapter.

The modern-day momentum of the prosperity gospel began in the 1950s.

Born in 1918, Granville "Oral" Roberts was, in many ways, the lead prosperity gospel pioneer of the modern era. He went from being a pastor to building a multimillion-dollar empire based on one major theological premise: God wants all people to be healthy and wealthy. Oral Roberts didn't mince words about his version of Jesus or the gospel. He adamantly taught and defended his belief that Jesus' highest wish is for us to prosper materially and have physical health equal to his peace and power in our souls.

Oral Roberts twisted the Bible to make his point. For instance, he taught that it was Jesus who said in 3 John 1:2, "Beloved, I wish above all things that thou mayest prosper and be in health, even as thy soul prospereth" (KJV). First, it was John who wrote this, not Jesus. Second, John is not telling Gaius (the recipient of the letter) that God wants him to be healthy and wealthy. This was merely the apostle John's loving way of greeting Gaius. John's greeting is comparable to sending an email that begins with, "Hi! I hope you're doing well." Being from a Middle Eastern family, I'm very familiar with the elaborate greetings and farewells of that culture. It is not uncommon for us to greet one another and say goodbye to each other with deep expressions like John used. This verse is not anything to build an entire religious position on. It's just a greeting!

Bestselling books by Oral Roberts often brought the two teachings of the prosperity gospel and the Word of Faith movement together under one roof. His books brandished catchy titles, such as *If You Need Healing Do These Things*, *The Miracle of Seed-Faith*, *A Daily Guide to Miracles*, and *Successful Living through Seed-Faith*. Desperate crowds could hardly resist his big promises. They ignored the fact that Roberts was butchering the true gospel of Jesus Christ. Big crowds and big money blinded both Roberts and those who followed him.

Meanwhile, the spread of the prosperity gospel was facilitated by numerous other factors, far too many to address here. But to shed some light for the reader, here are three to stir your thoughts:

1. *Technology*: Advancements in media enabled teachers to spread their version of the gospel faster than ever. From

America to Africa, global audiences were being swayed by the wrong gospel on prime-time television, mainstream radio, and nowadays, in the palms of their hands. The message preached so often appeared legitimate and appealed to their material needs. How can a missionary on the ground floor of the mission field compete with a Rolex-wearing preacher convincing people night after night that the gospel of health, wealth, and happiness made them rich?

2. *Seeker Movement:* For the past forty years, seeker-driven churches dominated the Christian landscape in America. A seeker-driven church is one that targets the interests of people who don't have an interest in church. This seems like a great idea, but the methods used to get people to come to church and keep people in church have little to do with the Bible. As the old saying goes, "How you get them in church is how you keep them in church." For the seeker-driven church, entertaining Broadway-style shows all but replaced the sermon, and secular music was played in worship to make non-Christians feel more comfortable. And can you guess what leaked into the message of these churches? The prosperity gospel. Jesus, in the seeker movement, was a blue-eyed white man who made your life better by providing the American dream. Seeker churches didn't talk about sin, repentance, or tough times. Hard truth (no matter how lovingly it was presented) was bad for business. A softer gospel meant softer messages. Everything was geared toward making people feel good. Like a friend who never tells you the hard truth, the seeker movement came up short in being faithful to preaching

all that Jesus taught. As a result, churches exploded with record attendance. People loved the seeker-driven Jesus because he was so easy to follow and offered a golden ticket to heaven. Caring for the flock of God by feeding them the truth became corporate pandering to keep people coming back. People weren't being challenged to grow deeper and exercise discernment. Instead, no matter how well-meaning the effort was, they sought unity at the cost of truth, and the results had dire consequences. Churches like Willow Creek openly admitted to creating biblically illiterate Christians for more than two decades before ever addressing it in 2008.[2] This is a microcosm of the bigger picture. Millions of Christians in America weren't being taught the Bible—they were being entertained. How could they stand against error unless they knew the truth? How could they take doctrine seriously if their leaders didn't? When would they know to stand for truth if their pastors avoided taking a stand?

3. *Compromising Consumerism:* Let's ask a really honest question here. How many prosperity preachers are now published by big name publishers? One major publisher had to pass on the manuscript for this book. Although they were interested, they would've had a storm of controversy on their hands because they have four globally recognized prosperity gospel authors who keep business booming. How many prosperity gospel books are on the shelves of major

---

2 Bob Burney, "Willow Creek Model, Its Leaders Say, Fails at Discipleship," Christianexaminer.com, January 1, 2008, https://www.christianexaminer.com/article/willow. creek.model.its.leaders.say.fails.at.discipleship/44056.htm.

Christian bookstores and retailers? How many conferences bring in famous preachers, even if they preach the prosperity gospel, because it fills the seats? Ultimately, this is highly lucrative to corporate Christian entities. Books, followers, products, and influence equal profit dollars. It's not the ideal, but it's the consumer-driven world we live in today.

Let me go one step farther than those three factors. This may sting a bit, but we need to rip the bandaid off here: we did this! By we, I mean all of us who profess to be Christians. We've collectively played some role in the rise of prosperity theology at some point. Whether by passive silence or active participation, we allow false gospels to get a footing. We need to take responsibility together, whether we believe we should or not, to eradicate evils like the prosperity gospel. That begins with committing ourselves to defending the true gospel at all costs.

How Far Does the Prosperity Gospel Reach?

The prosperity gospel used to be considered the cash cow of some fringe con artists posing as preachers. Today, the prosperity gospel has exploded to become one of the most popular teachings in the world. It has overtaken continents like Africa and South America as it continues to breed pastors and people who are looking to land a serious payday. It's now called the United States' number one export by Zambian pastor Conrad Mbewe, who has spent years dealing with the destruction that the prosperity gospel has wreaked in Africa.

Many of the largest churches and denominations in the US

over the last thirty years have focused their efforts so heavily on attracting and retaining members that they've paid little attention to what was going on outside their church or denominational circles. Therefore, the prosperity gospel was not collectively pushed back by the most popular and influential churches and denominations. There are highly influential churches that have pushed back, but they're a rarity. Perhaps many of them simply have chosen to ignore the threat, thinking it was only a few crazy televangelists on TBN. But now the prosperity gospel is everywhere.

Recently one of the last exclusively Christian orphan-sponsoring organizations in the world contacted me with one of the most humbling invitations I'd ever received. They wanted me to travel a few times a year, share my story, talk about the power of the gospel, and then help their organization by inviting people to sponsor poverty-stricken orphans around the world. I was so honored that they'd ask me to help, and had my assistant put a meeting with their representative on my calendar as soon as possible. Since in my former days I had spent so much time exploiting people in the third world, I jumped at the chance to help orphans through this ministry.

During our meeting, the representative explained the role, how the organization works, and what she'd like me to consider. Part of her pitch was telling me that they are the last organization offering orphan sponsorships that is exclusively Christian. An uncompromising parachurch ministry *and* they help orphans? I was all ears.

Things were progressing well until about thirty minutes into the meeting when the representative asked if I had any questions. I didn't have many, but I did ask who they work with. Though I was in the Hinn bubble for most of my life, we dabbled in mainstream evangelicalism and I knew the system very well—if you can make people money, they'll generally look the other way when it comes to certain things. I wanted to know if this global Christian organization was partnering with prosperity preachers.

After I posed the question, the meeting got awkward.

"So . . ." There was a pause. "We know how you feel about the prosperity gospel, but we did just sign a prosperity preacher to a deal because he's a big name and can help us get orphans sponsored."

"Why would your organization knowingly go down that road and then invite me to join? That makes no sense," I questioned. "Are you aware of how confusing that is going to be for people who know he's a prosperity preacher?"

"We completely understand, and I want you to know that we're asking that same big question as well. Our team has concerns, and we're seeking to address those."

The way that response came off seemed a lot like Christian corporate lingo for "we're trying to avoid a direct answer because we know we're compromising, but it's too late."

I nodded and expressed my unwillingness to share a stage with that prosperity preacher at any event for any joint purpose. I also told her I understood their wanting to do everything they could to help get orphans sponsored, but that bringing on prosperity preachers simply because they are a moneymaker is a slippery slope for a Christian organization to be on. The prosperity preachers exploit the third world, then get paid by the first world Christian organization to solicit sponsorships from Americans, who then sponsor the orphans in the third world. What an ecosystem! I wanted desperately to help them get orphans sponsored, but after our discussion, I wasn't sure they'd be following up with me or that I would feel good about working with them. I never did receive a phone call after that. I was not surprised.

Driving home from the meeting that day, I was so disturbed. What used to be called heresy by all of mainstream evangelicalism was now being overlooked. It seemed like everyone was muddying the waters and compromising classic, biblical, orthodox Christianity. Our faith was on the line. The world was watching as Christianity was being made a mockery of.

My joyous honeymoon in leaving the prosperity gospel behind was over. I quickly realized that compromise was going to be everywhere, even on what was supposed to be the good side. The Hinn family, along with other prosperity gospel empires, had done a very good job spreading the poison of prosperity theology far and wide.

The prosperity gospel is even changing the landscape of Latin America and the world's most Catholic country—Brazil. In a story for the *Washington Post*, Sarah Pulliam Bailey writes,

> Speaking from a stage encircled by twelve large wooden crosses, Gabriel Camargo held up wads of fake Brazilian money, showing his flock what could be theirs. "God will bless you if you give a lot more to the church," said Camargo, a pastor with the Universal Church of the Kingdom of God. Then he extended an arm and pointed a large black pouch toward his parishioners in the working-class neighborhood of Osasco. Pick up your wallets and purses, he said, instructing his flock to look for Brazilian reais. About a dozen people hurried forward, dumping bills and change into the bag. Those without cash didn't have to worry: An usher held out a credit

card machine. "You'll have so much money" by giving generously to the church, the pastor boomed, that "smoke is going
to come out of the machine." In a country struggling with
the worst economic crisis in its history, with long queues at
unemployment offices and public health clinics, perhaps it's
not surprising that Brazilians are increasingly drawn to the
promises of personal wealth.[3]

Nor is the American White House exempt. I received a call
one afternoon from a producer at CNN who asked me to join
Carol Costello on *Across America*. I had been on the show before,
but this time they needed a talking head on an embarrassing issue
for evangelicalism. Paula White, a known prosperity preacher and
the spiritual advisor to President Donald Trump, had just publicly
told people to give a special offering if they wanted God to bless
them. She even suggested that giving the offering would protect
them from divine consequences. This is nothing out of the ordinary for prosperity preachers, but with her public platform and
influence on how Christianity is represented in the White House,
it mattered immensely. After many pastors spoke up in outrage
and a series of news reports covered the story, a spokesperson for
Paula White went into damage control and released a statement
saying things were taken out of context. The statement conveyed
that Paula never intended for people to give out of fear of divine
judgment and that she was speaking more of her own commitment to give firstfruits to God. In my humble opinion, having

---

3 Sarah Pulliam Bailey, "How the Prosperity Gospel Is Sparking Major Change in the World's
Most Catholic Country," *Washington Post*, October 30, 2017, https://internationalreportingproject
.org/stories/view/how-the-prosperity-gospel-is-sparking-a-major-change-in-the-worlds-most-cat.

spent ample time with prosperity preachers and studying under them in the craft of fundraising, this was a classic example of going too far, then deflecting backlash. I believe the only thing taken out of context was Paula's interpretation of Scripture.

For now, the prosperity gospel is here to stay and is spanning the globe, doing damage to the true gospel of Jesus Christ. It is an evil that poses as blessing but is truly a curse. It appears to be a loving extension of God's goodness but is arguably the most hateful and abusive kind of false teaching plaguing the church today.

What Does the Bible Have to Say about False Teachers?

When one considers the prosperity gospel lifestyle and the teachers who propagate such damning doctrine, the implications can be overwhelming. People are losing their paychecks, their hope, and even their souls. Innocent people are being targeted by, at worst, charlatans who couldn't care less about the devastation they are causing so long as the dollars keep coming in, or by, at best, teachers who are seriously uneducated and unaware of basic biblical theology. At the same time, there seems to be a contingent of people who want this sort of teaching. Like the showman who climbs the stage to the roaring crowd's approval, there seems to be a sort of unwritten contract between the deceiver and the deceived. Could it be that people want prosperity preaching? Why do people fall for this sort of teaching? How can such evil go unchecked? Thankfully, the Bible provides answers to these questions. Let's look at four clear truths to help us dissect the lies:

1. *False teachers are disguised as good guys* (2 Cor. 11:13–15). When the apostle Paul was writing to the church at Corinth, their lack

of discernment was causing them to be led astray by false teachers who masqueraded as apostles of Christ (11:13), apparently to gain money, power, or both. The church was being poisoned by deceit, but they put up with it (11:4). Paul points out to the Corinthian church that he did not profit from his work with them; in fact, other churches funded his ministry in Corinth! But to make it clear that he is a true apostle and the others are false, he lists his credentials. Yes, he does signs, miracles, and wonders (12:12), but he never exploits anyone in his ministry, and he often suffers because of it (11:23–30). He has never taken advantage of them, enslaved or exploited them, or slapped them in the face,[4] as the false prophets have done (11:20). His effort was to help wake up the Corinthians to the trap being set for them. After pouring out his heart of love for the church and his concern that they are being led astray, Paul issues this warning: "For such men [those who preach a different gospel than Paul] are false apostles, deceitful workers, disguising themselves as apostles of Christ. No wonder, for even Satan disguises himself as an angel of light. Therefore it is not surprising if his servants also disguise themselves as servants of righteousness, whose end will be according to their deeds" (11:13–15).

The devil does not make it a habit to show up at the foot of your bed with his pitchfork and a red tail shouting, "Here I am to deceive you!" Likewise, his false prophets don't make their money by standing on the stage declaring, "Give all your money to my

---

4 Most commentators agree that this "slapping in the face" is likely a metaphorical reference to being disrespected, used, and treated with contempt. However, one can't help but notice the literal rendering of Paul's words and think of preachers mentioned earlier in the book, like Smith Wigglesworth, who physically assaulted sick people in his ministerial exploits.

greedy scheme and I'll give you false hope!" False prophets are like the Trojan horse—infiltrating the church from the inside. Like a Las Vegas casino, false prophets promise to give you all you ever dreamed of, then leave you with empty pockets. That is why Paul was so clear with these unsuspecting Corinthian Christians. It's life and death, and the devil is playing for keeps. We need to be discerning, aware, and biblically armed to resist deception no matter how good it looks, how good it sounds, or how good it promises to be.

2. *False teachers use deception to get rich* (2 Peter 2:1–3). Warning about the dangers that the church was facing, Peter wrote one of the most eye-opening letters when he penned 2 Peter. In it, he provides a perfect picture of what a false teacher will look like, and the motive behind their "ministry": "But false prophets also arose among the people, just as there will also be false teachers among you, who will secretly introduce destructive heresies, even denying the Master who bought them, bringing swift destruction upon themselves. Many will follow their sensuality, and because of them the way of the truth will be maligned; and in their greed they will exploit you with false words; their judgment from long ago is not idle, and their destruction is not asleep" (2 Peter 2:1–3).

Plain as day, Peter gives us the snapshot we need to understand what prosperity preachers are doing. They are Christ-mongers, twisting his name for gain and doing so "secretly" (v. 1). It's a drop of deception in the midst of truth. If they told 100 percent lies, they'd be caught. They are highly successful and able to sway "many" (v. 2) through their sensuality and smooth talk so as to go unnoticed in their predation of souls. Truth is ultimately sacrificed in order to achieve their main goal, and "in their greed they will exploit you with false words" (v. 3). Therein lies evidence of what the Bible means in saying that the love of money is the root of all sorts of evil (1 Tim. 6:10). It is this longing for money that drives false teachers to such extensive ends to obtain it. They don't make their money through honest work. Their work is to labor intensively for sordid gain, using a false front and a false Jesus to accomplish the task. Using the Greek word *plastos*, meaning artificial or fictitious, Peter gives us all we need to discern a false teacher's plastic veneer: (1) they'll subtly twist truths about Christ, (2) they'll be wildly popular, and (3) they will be greedy.

It doesn't matter how much truth they claim to believe or teach, if you see these three signs, the writing is on the wall.

3. *False teachers are in demand* (2 Tim. 4:3–5). It's not fair to blame only the greedy prosperity preachers. They wouldn't have a business if there weren't so many demanding customers. In his final letter, Paul warned his pastoral protege, Timothy, about the way things were going to get, and it wasn't going to be pretty. He cautioned, "For the time will come when they will not endure sound doctrine; but wanting to have their ears tickled, they will accumulate for themselves teachers in accordance to their own desires, and will turn away their ears from the truth and will turn aside to myths. But you, be sober in all things, endure hardship, do the work of an evangelist, fulfill your ministry" (2 Tim. 4:3–5).

Like a mob calling for the verdict of their choice, there are people who truly want the prosperity gospel.

Paul was warning about people who prefer myths to the truth because of how good the myths make them feel. Churches today are filled with this sort of exchange. Pastors take the pulpits and tell people what they want to hear and send them out feeling good every week. One wrong word or tough-love sermon? They're leaving and taking their checkbooks with them.

Who in their right mind would go to a doctor if they only ever received good news? Shouldn't patients be told if there is something wrong too? If their symptoms are grim, should a doctor not provide an accurate diagnosis and treat the problem? No patient tells the doctor, "How dare you tell me truth! I'm out of here!" Yet we prefer that our pastors avoid the topic of sin, tell us God wants us all rich and happy, and then send us out into the hostile world with a pat on the back, saying, "You're good." Not on Paul's watch! He wanted young Timothy to understand that while some people want it easy, the real church will want the hard truth because they will want to change for the better. They will want to face their sin, they will want to know God's will for their lives, and they will want to know if they are wrong so they can be made right.

The demand for easy believism and religious roulette will always be there, but it doesn't mean we need to fall into the trap.

4. *False teachers will get what they deserve (Jude 12–13)*. Whenever I talk with people about the perils of the prosperity gospel, there is almost always a person who remarks, "I hope those people burn in hell. They deserve it." Such sentiments should never be tossed around casually. God has the final say on when they will take their final breath, and our job is not to determine what a man or woman deserves but rather to live in obedience to God and beg that he change them. As sinners, we all deserve hell (Rom. 3:23), but by repenting of our sins and turning to Jesus Christ in faith, we can be saved (Rom. 10:9). For now, while we are still living, the Bible gives fair warning about the destruction awaiting abusive false teachers. Jude says, "These are the men who are hidden reefs in your love feasts when they feast with you without fear, caring for themselves; clouds without water, carried along by

winds; autumn trees without fruit, doubly dead, uprooted; wild waves of the sea, casting up their own shame like foam; wandering stars, for whom the black darkness has been reserved forever" (Jude 12–13).

With poetic yet vividly literal imagery, Jude writes what we can identify today in the lives of prosperity preachers. They are like shepherds who feed themselves richly as they live like royalty on the backs of those in the gutter. They are like clouds without water and dead trees because they appear to be something but produce nothing of value or nourishment. Their lifestyles are marked by deception, greed, prostitution, immorality, molestation, felony, mockery, and abuse of the most vulnerable in our world today.

The apostle Peter also sternly warns about false teachers. "But these, like unreasoning animals, born as creatures of instinct to be captured and killed, reviling where they have no knowledge, will in the destruction of those creatures also be destroyed, suffering wrong as the wages of doing wrong. They count it a pleasure to revel in the daytime. They are stains and blemishes, reveling in their deceptions, as they carouse with you, having eyes full of adultery that never cease from sin, enticing unstable souls, having a heart trained in greed, accursed children" (2 Peter 2:12–14).

None of this should make us smile or reach for our gavel. We are not God's police administering his justice and condemning souls with an authority that only he possesses. This should cause us to answer the following question with tearful sobriety: how can they get away with this?

When God's Word says that the "black darkness has been reserved" (Jude 13), that means exactly what you think it means. You could even go as far as saying that the hottest part of hell is reserved for those who twist the name of Jesus Christ and lead people there. Not one will get away with it. That reality should break our hearts and cause us to pray for the repentance of those who are caught in the snares of the prosperity gospel, especially its teachers.

Why Is the Prosperity Gospel So Dangerous?

One of the reasons that people are blind to the dangers of the prosperity gospel is they are blissfully unware of just how anti-Christian it is. If we truly understand how evil it is, it isn't difficult to see the satanic nature of it and the reason why every church, every pastor, and every Christian should stand against it. Volumes have been written about this topic, but I've done my best to boil it all down to a top-ten list that you can use when navigating this subject with friends and family. Each item on the list contrasts some biblical truths with prosperity gospel deception.

1. *The prosperity gospel distorts the biblical gospel.* The biblical gospel can be properly understood by looking at some gospel-saturated passages. In Romans 5:8–10, Paul declares, "But God demonstrates His own love toward us, in that while we were yet sinners, Christ died for us. Much more then, having now been justified by His blood, we shall be saved from the wrath of God through Him. For if while we were enemies we were reconciled to God through the death of His Son, much more, having been reconciled, we shall be saved by His life."

In Romans 3:23–25, we read that sin is something we all have committed, and that the glory of God is something we all fall short of. Paul writes, "For all have sinned and fall short of the glory of God, being justified as a gift by His grace through the redemption which is in Christ Jesus; whom God displayed publicly as a propitiation in His blood through faith. This was to demonstrate His righteousness, because in the forbearance of God He passed over the sins previously committed."

Finally, in what is perhaps the most comprehensive gospel passage in the entire Bible, Ephesians 2:4–10 contains explosively truthful statements regarding what God accomplished in Christ and what our purpose is in this life. Paul writes, "But God, being rich in mercy, because of His great love with which He loved us, even when we were dead in our transgressions, made us alive together with Christ (by grace you have been saved), and raised us up with Him, and seated us with Him in the heavenly places in Christ Jesus, so that in the ages to come He might show the surpassing riches of His grace in kindness toward us in Christ Jesus. For by grace you have been saved through faith; and that not of yourselves, it is the gift of God; not as a result of works, so that no one may boast. For we are His workmanship, created in Christ Jesus for good works, which God prepared beforehand so that we would walk in them."

When you look at these passages, what do you notice? Is the gospel about the gifts or the Giver? Is the gospel about the redeemed or the Redeemer? Is the gospel about earthly riches or eternal reward? Is the gospel about monetary gain or the glory of God? Is the gospel about obtaining my materialistic desires or using what I have to do good works for God? I bet, if you're a biblically discerning Christian, you answered those questions correctly.

The prosperity gospel distorts the biblical gospel by making the Good News all about you and all about stuff. The abundant life of John 10:10 is smeared to mean that God's will is for you to have Bentleys, mansions, and job promotions. I've got news for you—no, actually, I've got *good* news for you: the abundant life is about the security of your soul for eternity. The abundant life is not a comfortable seventy years, courtesy of the prosperity gospel and leading to infinite suffering in hell if you don't follow the biblical Christ as your Savior.

2. *The prosperity gospel insults God's nature.* God is divinely infinite and beyond our human comprehension. Still, he has made himself known to us through divine revelation (Scripture) and his Son, Jesus Christ. His attributes are such that he is beyond human control. He cannot be made into a formula. He cannot be manipulated. He is holy, the definition of perfection. He is eternal; time cannot hold him. He is sovereign, the majestic ruler of the universe.

Psalm 115:3 reminds us, "But our God is in the heavens; He does whatever He pleases." Job said, "Naked I came from my mother's womb, and naked I shall return there. The Lord gave and the Lord has taken away. Blessed be the name of the Lord" (Job 1:21). John 4:24 minces no words: "God is spirit, and those who worship Him must worship in spirit and truth." We have to realize that God's nature is not something we manipulate; it's something we must submit to.

In stark contrast to this truth, the prosperity gospel teaches that God can, like a cosmic magic genie, grant our wishes. The prosperity gospel teaches a version of the nature of God that is so skewed it scarcely communicates one iota of who he is. This is dangerous and abusive because it does not introduce people to their Creator, whom they desperately need to know. His love is not bought, and his blessings are free. His servants are ambassadors who represent who he really is.

3. *The prosperity gospel confuses the atonement.* The atonement can be defined simply as what Jesus did when he went to the cross, bore our sins, and conquered death by rising from the grave (1 John 2:2). To atone for something means you pay for it and make amends. Jesus provided redemption for lost sinners like you and me. He was the atonement lamb who paid the penalty for our sins.

The benefits of the atonement are eternal, but the joy of expectation can be experienced on earth. For example, Jesus died for our sins and gave us eternal life, but we're not living eternally—yet (John 3:16). Jesus promised his disciples that he would prepare a place for them (John 14:3), and that everyone who sacrifices to follow him will receive one hundredfold and eternal life (Matt. 19:29), but is everyone getting their hundredfold yet? No. Furthermore, the atonement provides for a heaven with no sickness, no tears, no sin, and no pain (Rev. 21:4), but on this earth are we all disease free, sinless, never to cry again or wince in pain? No. Finally, the atonement means that those who inherit everlasting life in heaven will receive a glorified body (1 Cor. 15:42–53), but are we floating around in glorified spirit-bodies yet? Again, no.

Prosperity preachers write checks with their mouths that the Bible doesn't cash. They use and abuse the atonement to mean that God guarantees your healing because of the atonement for your soul. Worse, they promise that Jesus' death on the cross didn't provide just eternal life; it provides earthly riches. All you have to do is, by faith, tap into those things he already paid for. This is a damaging lie that takes something beautiful about our Savior's work on the cross and turns it into a petty transaction for fleeting pleasures.

4. *The prosperity gospel demeans Jesus Christ.* Paul says, "To live is Christ and to die is gain" (Phil. 1:21). John the Baptist says, "He must increase, but I must decrease" (John 3:30). Over and over the Bible expresses the glory of Jesus Christ as the be-all and end-all for the Christian. Jesus is the radiance of God's glory and sustainer of all things (Heb. 1:3), whoever has Jesus has life (1 John 5:12), and he is the only way to heaven (John 14:6). Without Jesus, heaven would be hell. All the health and wealth this world can offer can never compare to the vast riches of abiding with the Son of God for all eternity. Jesus is everything. The prosperity gospel makes human satisfaction to be material and Jesus to be the cherry on top. If it makes Jesus a central focus, it's that he is the main avenue to getting what you want. This version of Jesus is a shell of who he really is. The prosperity gospel promises people the abundant life that Jesus offers only to deliver a gospel with no Jesus at all.

5. *The prosperity gospel twists Scripture.* The Bible is a big book and can seem really intimidating. But upon investigation, we find out it is simple to understand if we approach it the right way. The Bible is a compilation of Spirit-inspired writings by authors, to an audience, with applications. For example, when we read Paul's letter to the Ephesians, we need to keep in mind the intent of his letter and what his audience was experiencing at that time. Only then, and after we've properly understood those things, can we effectively apply the Scriptures to our lives today. It's never a wise plan to read things into the Bible that aren't in the text. It's also never a wise plan to say things about the gospel that the Bible doesn't say.

James 3:1 is a sobering reminder for those who teach the Bible. James writes, "Let not many of you become teachers, my brethren, knowing that as such we will incur a stricter judgment." The prosperity gospel takes the age-old interpretative strategies that scholars have used for generations and turns them upside-down. The rules for hermeneutics (how to interpret Scripture) are tossed out the window! It takes passages that are plain in meaning based on what they literally say in Scripture and makes them to mean something completely different. Like an evil imposter taking a heartfelt letter from a king to his royal subjects and twisting it for self-serving purposes it was never intended to be used for, prosperity preachers take the Bible and twist it into a tool for abuse.

6. *The prosperity gospel is motivated by love for money.* Money is like a microscope, magnifying what's really going on inside of us. God, knowing that money would be no small issue in the hearts of human beings, gave instructions in the Bible for both using it well if you do have it, and keeping the right perspective if you don't. Proverbs is full of wisdom that can save you a lot of health and-wealth-gospel headaches. As it notes, wisdom is better than riches (Prov. 3:13), so it's worth paying close attention to what the Bible says. Trusting in riches does little good (Prov. 11:28), money gained by deception doesn't last (Prov. 10:2), and it's better to have a little but keep your integrity (Prov. 16:8). Beyond Proverbs, the Bible says that the love of money is the root of all kinds of evil (1 Tim. 6:10). The prosperity gospel is obsessed with money and material gain. To argue that is to argue that gravity does not exist. It's a fact that we need to keep in mind when we're tempted to buy in to the lies. Nothing good comes from the love of money.

7. *The prosperity gospel produces false converts.* If the prosperity gospel Jesus is not the real Jesus, and the prosperity gospel is not the real gospel, and many people chasing the prosperity gospel aren't

real Christians, then what is going on? Without broad-brushing every human soul who is involved in the prosperity gospel, it is no stretch to say that there are millions of false converts in the world today who think they are saved, but they are being deceived. That's why our mission is so vital. Jesus is not done changing lives, but he uses people to present the truth to other people. He said if we love him, we will obey him (John 14:23), and that knowing the truth brings freedom (John 8:32). The prosperity gospel fills pulpits with imposters and the pews with people who either want to be fooled (2 Tim. 4:3) or are being deceived (2 Tim. 3:13). This kind of bondage is not evidence of Christ's involvement and makes for a messy situation both inside and outside the church. Nor is this confusion the mark of the Holy Spirit. The Holy Spirit's resume shows a faithful track record of guiding us into truth (John 16:13).

8. *The prosperity gospel overcomplicates faith.* When it comes to our salvation, faith is a monumentally important thing to understand. Our salvation, our faith, and our ability to do good works on this earth are all gifts from God (Eph. 2:8–10). Having faith in Jesus Christ is what saves us, and the evidence of that faith being genuine is a life that follows after him. Jesus doesn't make being his follower complicated. Though it may not be an easy life, it is a life full of freedom in him! He promises that his yoke is easy and his burden is light (Matt. 11:30), and that his people can cast their anxieties on him because he cares (1 Peter 5:7).

Faith isn't giving money to get his love. Faith isn't paying a fee for his saving grace. Faith isn't going broke to get healed. Faith isn't traveling to a special service to get his anointing. Faith is repenting of your sins and turning to him, believing that he is the Son of God. Any religion that says you need to do good works, give enough money, or speak enough positive declarations to unlock God's saving grace or abundant blessings on your life is a false religion. Christian faith is believing in Jesus Christ for eternal life and experiencing the joy, freedom, and blessing of knowing Christ for free!

The prosperity gospel turns faith into a works-based system and confuses it by adding burdens that people cannot carry. The Pharisees did the same thing when they were manipulating and exploiting people (Luke 11:46).

9. *The prosperity gospel ruins Christianity's witness.* Jesus said, "So then, none of you can be My disciple who does not give up all his own possessions" (Luke 14:33), to make his point that worship of stuff is not the mark of his followers. Yet the prosperity gospel worships material goods, and the world knows it. The prosperity gospel couldn't be worse for our Christian witness. Men and women who preach the prosperity gospel on Sunday are laughing all the way to the bank on Monday. The world looks on as it makes a mockery of Jesus, the pastoral leaders of the church, and the Bible as the foundation we stand on for teaching. Unfortunately, many people are leaving the church because of this abuse of power. Christian leaders are expected to be free from the love of money (1 Tim. 3:3), not obsessing over how to raid the offering buckets. Christian leaders are expected to care for people as loving, humble shepherds (1 Peter 5:2), not act as manipulative salesmen. Finally, Christian leaders are expected to use their God-given authority to protect people from deception and boldly steer the church into truth (Heb. 13:17), not exploit and control desperate people.

10. *The prosperity gospel abuses vulnerable people.* The prosperity gospel attracts those who are looking to get rich off of people

desperate for hope. What these desperate, vulnerable people need is a pastor who will love them, protect them, and give them real hope. Too many churches are being overrun by charlatans, and the church at large has got to say, "Enough is enough." Vulnerable people should be targeted by the church for the purpose of serving their spiritual and physical needs, not squeezing every dollar out of them in exchange for empty promises.

Prosperity gospel preaching must be outlawed across evangelicalism, and those who preach it and partner with it should be avoided. It's time for Christianity to send the message that the prosperity gospel will not poison our witness and win over the hearts of the hurting. We must stand firm in our faith and trust the truth to win the day. That starts by telling the truth, no matter how uncomfortable that may be. True healing can begin when we've got the right diagnosis. The prosperity gospel is a disease.

10

A Balanced View on Health and Wealth

Abundance isn't God's provision for me
to live in luxury. It's his provision for me to
help others live. God entrusts me with his
money not to build my kingdom on earth,
but to build his kingdom in heaven.

—RANDY ALCORN

A dear friend of mine has been immensely blessed with the ability to gain wealth. He's a hard worker, a man of integrity, and everything he touches seems to turn to gold.

Almost whispering, he asked me one time, "Is it okay that I make so much money?" He explained that his employer wanted to give him another raise as a reward for his work ethic and impact on the company. He was considering turning it down because he felt like it was too much money for one person to make. After a brief discussion, it became obvious that his problem wasn't making too much money; his problem was fear of being labeled as greedy because he was wealthy.

Our conversation provoked a study of the Scriptures to discover what God has to say on the subject. Is God opposed to a Christian making a high salary? What's wrong with an employer rewarding an employee for doing his job? Should Christians take a vow of poverty and purposely try to suffer? Is poverty God's will for us?

For all the damage done by the prosperity gospel over the past few decades, the "poverty gospel" has made itself a sinister force too. Some Christians think that deliberately suffering or living below the poverty line makes them more spiritual. They wear their asceticism like a badge of honor, boasting about how little they make their families live on and how hard they make their own lives by doing so. Bragging about not buying shoes (when you can) or using a verse about rich people not getting into heaven to excuse yourself from being a steward is no better than a prosperity preacher living on the other side of the spectrum.

Many Christians have become wary of wealth or hide their questions about money for fear of being labeled a prosperity gospel propagator. I've met Christians who are scared to pray for physical healing because people may think they're in the health-and-wealth-gospel fan club. To this line of thinking, I say two things: (1) We have to relentlessly call the prosperity gospel what it is: evil. (2) We have to maintain biblical balance in our understanding of health and wealth. Remember, God is a Father who cares about the details of our lives (Luke 12:7), and that means his Word has much to say about our physical and material needs. The prosperity gospel fools people by mixing some of God's truth into their poisonous theological concoction. We cannot start being fearful of biblical teachings on money or healing because a prosperity gospel preacher overemphasizes them. We simply need to keep our biblical balance.

In this chapter, I've outlined some basic biblical principles for you to consider when it comes to health and wealth, and I encourage you to expand on these and dig deeper. My prayer is that these truths will help you as you navigate your convictions and circumstances. Whether you are struggling to make ends meet and just received a negative diagnosis, or you are a gospel patron who is giving away millions for kingdom advancement and enjoying perfect health, the Bible will keep you from tipping the scales too far to one extreme.

The Bible on Health

Principle 1: God still heals today. No matter how careful a Christian may be on their position on healing gifts, both cessationists (believing certain gifts have ceased) and continuists (believing all gifts continue today) must agree that, biblically speaking, God still heals today. The Bible gives a clear picture of what the church should be: a vibrant community of faith led by qualified leaders who are anxious for nothing, thankful, prayerful, and full of peace (Phil. 4:6–7). We ought to trust God with our prayers, knowing that he heals according to his will and purposes. His sovereign hand in healing moves in his own time. Sometimes people are sick for years before experiencing healing. Other times, people seem to pray just once and receive a healing. Sometimes he uses a doctor to heal. Sometimes, people do not get healed on earth, but they will be free of sickness and pain for all eternity in heaven (Rev. 21:4). In every circumstance, God is a healer. It's just not always his will to heal right now, on earth. When and how he heals is up to him.

Principle 2: Health isn't guaranteed on earth. If being a Christian guarantees that you will have health, then either there is something wrong with tens of millions of Christians around the world or there is something wrong with that line of thinking. I'd offer that there is little wrong with them and would even go farther to say that the physical limitations and trials of this life are normal. Yes, there are times when sin is linked to sickness (James 5:13–16), and there may be rare occurrences when demons can be linked to sickness (Luke 13:11), but overall, sickness is a part of life on a broken earth. We can thank God for creating our bodies to fight sickness and recover on their own, for medical science that in many instances helps restore the body, and for the trials that make us stronger and cause us to lean on Jesus, experiencing his comfort in ways we never thought possible (Ps. 34:18).

Principle 3: Christian joy is not dependent on circumstances. Over the past few months, our church has done four funerals. One was for a precious full-term, stillborn baby girl. Another was for a fifty-eight-year-old father of three whose wife was battling cancer. About two months after he passed, his wife passed away also. Then, just about a month after that, we received a phone call that a faithful, dedicated twenty-three-year-old young man in our church was killed by a driver who'd run a red light. Our church was shaken to its core.

These families were devastated. Yet in the midst of all the loss, they still found reasons to praise God. Nobody was happy about these painful losses, but how in the world was everybody still able to find joy? Why did the grieving families call the funeral services a "graduation" or a "celebration" of life? In the midst of tragedy, how could they speak of triumph? But they did. One by one, through all of the tears, these families put their faith on display by proving that Christian joy is not dependent on circumstances. They spoke of their eternal perspective and rejoiced over the assurance of salvation for their loved ones because of faith in Jesus (John 14:6). The Holy Spirit's fruit was evident in their lives through joy (Gal. 5:22), and thus brought even more assurance of his presence and peace. God was glorified as they counted the results of their trials joyful because God strengthened, proved, and used their faith to be a witness to everyone around them (Rom. 5:3–5; James 1:2).

None of this talk about joy means that there isn't pain. Nor is this some religious coping mechanism to avoid reality. No, Christians do not count it joyful to experience trials in this life—it is the results that we find joy in. God is at work, making our pain matter and using our stories to encourage and strengthen someone else. That is still good (Rom. 8:28).

Principle 4: Suffering and trials are a part of life. No matter how wonderful we believe this world should be, and no matter how perfect a prosperity preacher says your life will be if you give a big enough offering, suffering and trials are a part of life. Ask around or reflect on your life right now. Have you gotten sick? Lost a loved one? Been hurt by others? Been lied about and accused of things you never did? Been abused? Rejected? Of course. We all have in one way or another. Jesus promised that in this world there will be trouble (John 16:33), that you will be hated if you follow him (Matt. 10:22), and that families will divide over him (Matt. 10:34–36). The Bible even says that all who desire to live godly lives in Christ Jesus will be persecuted (2 Tim. 3:12). But Jesus also promised rest for weary souls (Matt. 11:28–30) and a peace that this world cannot give (John 14:27).

The Bible paints a beautiful picture for the Christian who endures suffering and trials. No matter what we go through, nothing can separate us from God's love (Rom. 8:38–39), and he'll provide us ways to escape temptations along the way (1 Cor. 10:13). God has a glorious future prepared for those who love him and remain faithful (1 Cor. 2:9).

Principle 5: Physical limitations do not limit ministry impact. Paul preached when his body was failing him (Gal. 4:13), and he ministered when he was being tormented and feeling weak and defeated (2 Cor. 12:7). Yet God by his grace worked through Paul's weakness (2 Cor. 12:9). Just like Paul, we aren't limited by the fact that God doesn't always heal when we demand he does.

Joni Eareckson Tada is a quadriplegic who has used the hope of Jesus Christ to help her live for his glory. For fifty years now, Joni has been confined to a wheelchair. Her story is one of difficulty and tears. She doesn't zip around in her wheelchair excited to be a quad. She doesn't relish in it and make herself out to be some happy-to-be-handicapped individual. She has told audiences numerous times how she has struggled at various times through the years to find the will to live. Yet in it all, she presses on, ministering to thousands through her books, speeches, and Joni and Friends ministry. She lives one day at a time, determined to let God give her strength, peace, and meaning no matter her situation.

You can probably think of people in your life who have lived like this. Maybe a mother who fought cancer but never stopped changing the world with her love. Maybe a friend who had every right to feel sorry for himself because he was sick yet selflessly took care of others with lesser needs. God uses ordinary people to do extraordinary things, and that often includes those others would consider weak. Prosperity preachers miss out on one of the greatest privileges of the gospel when they live in a bubble of false hope: real hope for real people as the real gospel transforms lives through their ministry.

The Bible on Wealth

Money tests our hearts like little else on earth. Whether it be the test of poverty or the test of prosperity, money brings out the best and worst in us. Far too often, and I am sure you'd agree, we're afraid to admit we don't know as much about managing money as we ought to. Within church circles, it's even more daunting to face our deficiencies on money management because we're supposed to be people of the Book with all of the answers rolling off the tips of our tongues. Reality is, everybody needs to continuously revisit biblical principles on money and be a lifelong student of financial stewardship. To help contrast some of the bad teaching out there, here are some starter principles to build on. Check out the recommended resources page in the back of this book for books or programs that helped me rebuild a biblically balanced view on wealth.

Principle 1: *God owns everything.* When we think of wealth, first we have to understand that God owns everything! God doesn't owe you and me anything, he isn't shocked by the state of the world, and he never "lost the deed to the earth" when Adam sinned, as prosperity preachers and Word of Faith enthusiasts will preach. God doesn't just hold the deed to all land, he is the Creator of all land.

God owns the cattle on a thousand hills (Ps. 50:10); he owns everything under heaven, for that matter (Job 41:11). The psalmist declares, "The earth is the LORD's, and all it contains, the world, and those who dwell in it" (Ps. 24:1). There is no arguing with the Bible on who owns everything. God does.

So if God is the owner of everything, what does that make us? When we understand this first principle, we quickly realize we are simply managers. One day, we'll give an account for how we've managed what he's entrusted to us (Matt. 25:14–30).

Principle 2: Wealth isn't guaranteed on earth. The Bible is equally as clear that while God owns everything, wealth isn't guaranteed for everyone on earth. Jesus told his disciples that the poor would always be with them (John 12:8). We can gather from his words that people are naturally going to struggle financially in this broken world. No wonder Scripture is so adamant that the poor be cared for—they are some of society's most vulnerable people. Assuming, of course, that they are not poor because they are lazy (the Bible has much to say on laziness, but we'll have to cover that another time), God cares greatly for those who are in need. The book of Proverbs contains wisdom on serving the poor because wealth is not always going to be evenly spread around the world. Because of that, we should:

- Not oppress the poor but rather be kind to them (Prov. 14:31)
- Lend to the poor and trust the Lord with the results (Prov. 19:17)
- Be generous and share food with the poor (Prov. 22:9)
- Give to the poor and not ignore them (Prov. 28:27)
- Protect the rights of the poor (Prov. 29:7)

Caring for the poor is necessary because wealth is not guaranteed for all. Beyond that, Scripture shows us what God wants for all of us. Contentment, not riches, should be the goal of every believer. We must maintain balance in our understanding on wealth and poverty. With his intelligence, extensive religious training (Acts 26:5), and Roman citizenship (Acts 22:27), the apostle Paul was certainly deserving of great wealth, but clearly he missed out on whatever the prosperity preachers of today are selling. On the topic of the haves and the have-nots, Paul writes, "I know how to get along with humble means, and I also know how to live in prosperity; in any and every circumstance I have learned the secret of being filled and going hungry, both of having abundance and suffering need" (Phil. 4:12).

God accomplishes his purposes in and through both the poor and the rich. In the end, contentment is the key to a happy heart (1 Tim. 6:8).

Principle 3: *Wealth is a tool for gospel advancement.* Even though wealth is not guaranteed on earth, God does give the opportunity to gain wealth. You may say, "Nobody gave me wealth—I earned it!" The children of Israel thought the same thing, but Moses reminded them that it was God who was blessing them based solely on his sovereign will. Deuteronomy 8:17–18 says, "You may say in your heart, 'My power and the strength of my hand made me this wealth.' But you shall remember the LORD your God, for it is He who is giving you power to make wealth, that He may confirm His covenant which He swore to your fathers, as it is this day." If God has blessed you with wealth, you ought to humbly thank him and realize that you have a great responsibility. Speaking to the rich, John writes, "But whoever has the world's goods, and sees his brother in need and closes his heart against him, how does the love of God abide in him? Little children, let us not love with word or with tongue, but in deed and truth" (1 John 3:17–18).

The Bible is hardly silent on what rich people are supposed to do with all that money. Sure, it's biblical and prudent to leave an inheritance for your children (Prov. 13:22), and it's good to work hard and save for the future (Prov. 6:6). But you know what the greatest purpose of wealth is? To advance the gospel and do God's will! Paul told Timothy that rich people are to do this very thing. In a straightforward passage, he says, "Instruct those who are rich in this present world not to be conceited or to fix their hope on the uncertainty of riches, but on God, who richly supplies us with all things to enjoy. Instruct them to do good, to be rich in good works, to be generous and ready to share, storing up for themselves the treasure of a good foundation for the future, so that they may take hold of that which is life indeed" (1 Tim. 6:17–19).

There you have it. Wealth is not a sin. You're allowed to enjoy it. But don't for a second fix your hope on it. It's a tool for ministry, not materialism.

Jesus offered one of the best investment strategies in the universe when he said to store up treasure in heaven where nothing can destroy it (Matt. 6:19–21). This is done by putting your resources to gospel-centered use.

You can't take it with you. There will be no U-Haul behind the hearse.

Principle 4: *Wealth is not a sign of elite spiritual status.* Prosperity preachers will tell you that wealth is a sign of an elite spiritual awakening. As in, "You have finally realized your full identity as a child of God when you step into the wealth God has for you." Or some nonsense like that.

Again, check the Bible on this. It is estimated the Bible contains upward of two thousand references to money. Approximately 50 percent of Jesus' parables deal with stewardship of money and things, and nearly three hundred verses in just the gospels alone deal with money. Doesn't this tell you that money and wealth are a serious subject to God? Nor do all of these verses contain exciting affirmations about being wealthy; rather, many of them contain warnings about being wealthy. Wealth is often a distraction from what really matters, so it takes a lot of discipline and biblical teaching to keep your heart from being sucked in by money's malicious pull. The wealthy are often in a tug-of-war between their affection for earthly things (Phil. 3:19) and the eternal life to come. Wealthy believers, by the power of the Holy Spirit, can overcome temptation and use wealth as a tool for good, but more than likely there will always be a battle in the heart between giving generously and the natural inclination to keep, keep, keep.

Does the Bible paint wealth as a mark of the spiritual elite, or does it warn of the dangers of having all the things your heart desires? Look at what the Bible warns about wealth and decide for yourself:

- You can't serve two masters (Matt. 6:24).
- The deceitfulness of riches chokes out fruitfulness (Mark 4:19).
- It's difficult for rich people to choose Christ over wealth (Luke 18:22–23).
- It's difficult for rich people to enter the kingdom of God (Luke 18:25).
- The love of money is the root of all evil (1 Tim. 6:10).
- Your soul is your most important asset (Luke 12:20).
- You can gain the whole world yet lose your soul if you do not have Christ (Mark 8:36).

In the Bible, the poor and afflicted are given special attention when it comes to spiritual care, and they often are able to worship more freely because they are free of the entanglements of riches. Revelation 2:9 illustrates this perfectly and tells us what real riches are. Jesus calls the church of Smyrna rich because even though they are in poverty and tribulation, they have held fast to their faith no matter the cost. They receive the highly esteemed crown of life for their faithfulness and suffering on earth (Rev. 2:10). Paul said that he considered anything he gained as loss for the sake of Christ and that all things are loss compared with knowing Christ Jesus (Phil. 3:7–8). What a powerful truth! Wealth is not a sign of elite spiritual status—having Christ is.

Don't buy the lies the prosperity preachers sell. You and I are going to be surprised one day when heaven's "Hall of Faith" is not lined with bigwigs and wealthy executives. Rather, it will be filled with the poor who gave what they could but never had what we have. They will have stood for their faith but paid with their lives. They will have been the nameless and faceless here on earth, but God will call them faithful.

Principle 5: Wealth is an immense responsibility. If you're wealthy, you were meant to build God's kingdom, not your earthly empire. Jesus said not to be anxious about any kind of provision but instead to seek his kingdom and his righteousness and that everything else will be taken care of (Matt. 6:31–33). We are all called to live generous lives with whatever means we have. Jesus said that when a widow gave two cents, she had given more than the wealthy who had given large amounts (Luke 21:1–4). He doesn't see the size of our gifts; he sees the state of our hearts. When we give, we must give willingly, not under compulsion (2 Cor. 8:12; 9:7). Wealth is to be stewarded, trusting that God has blessed us to be a blessing and that he will keep blessing us as he sees fit. Our job isn't to keep; our job is to work hard, invest, and give generously (again, see Matt. 25:14–30).

Prosperity gospel preachers want you to give to them to make them rich, but God wants you to give to faithful gospel ministries to help them reach. There is a world of hurting and broken people, and money can make a huge impact in ways that will long outlive you. You will be accountable for how you managed the wealth God has given you. That is an immense responsibility. What will your conversation be like before the throne of Christ? Will you stammer and stutter, claiming to have tried to give a little here and there while you spent most of it on your own pleasures and let the poor suffer and the church struggle? Or will you joyfully report to the Master, saying, "Lord, sometimes it went against the grain of this world to give sacrificially for your work, but pleasing you was the priceless treasure I held on to!" If we live that way, I have no doubt we will hear, "Well done, good and faithful slave. You were faithful with a few things, I will put you in charge of many things; enter into the joy of your master" (Matt. 25:23).

A few years ago, I had the privilege of heading across the border to Mexico with a group from our church to do some missions work and build a home for a family experiencing extreme poverty. The family of five lived in the slums of Tijuana. When we pulled up to the small lot to begin the project, I was floored by the way they lived—yet they were so happy. There was hardly a bathroom in sight, and the one we were offered was not much more than a makeshift hole in the ground and a bucket for washing up. Children played soccer in the dirt surrounded by shacks made of tin, scrap, and plywood. These kids were oblivious to the fact that we had just traveled from one of the richest counties in the US. They weren't looking for an Xbox, complaining about their iPads needing to be charged, or telling their moms their shoes were out of style. Most of them didn't even have shoes.

As the days went by, we continued to meet families and children who embodied what it means to be joyfully content. When we completed the home, it was little more than a wooden box on top of concrete, but they acted like we had built them the Ritz-Carlton!

The family fed us like kings each day, and at the end of the weeklong trip, our group leader told us that the family had spent one month's salary to feed our group. Some of our members began to cry and beg the host to let us pay back the money they'd spent on feeding us. The family refused any such payment. Why?

The mother of the family spoke up in Spanish as we all gathered around the inside of the home and held hands to pray that final day. Through a translator we were told that for them, the joy of giving and providing hospitality had far outweighed the sacrifice they had made to do so. There wasn't a dry eye as we prayed that day. Clearly, giving generously is not reserved for only the wealthy.

So go ahead! Work hard, enjoy life, and celebrate the gifts that God has given you. Be content, seek his kingdom first, care for others, and give generously in whatever ways he has enabled you to do. In all your working, living, striving, giving, and caring, remember to maintain biblical balance and keep eternity in mind.

God is not trying to take away all you have—he's the one who gave it. He is, more than anything, testing the affections of your heart and offering you a joy beyond this world with him in glory.

Wealth is not a sin; it's a responsibility. Use it well.

11

How to Reach Those Caught in Deception

Your greatest ability is your availability.

—UNKNOWN

Like generations throughout church history, we need to be focused on taking the truth to those who have never heard it before. Yet today, as apostasy increases and seemingly faithful men and women go rogue theologically, we'll need not only outreach (to those who've never heard the gospel) but "inreach" (to those believing in a false Christ). Yes, many are getting the ear-tickling teachers they desire (2 Tim. 4:3–4), but within the masses of apostates, there are sheep who need to be rescued.

We're faced with the tall task of evangelism within our ranks. One moment, we see a glimmer of hope in someone we try to reach, only to experience another moment of sorrow when someone we love is swept up in deceit. Maybe you've ruined a few Thanksgiving dinners trying to tell people how it is, or held personal crusades during a lunch break at work. In the end, many Christians who are trying to reach those caught in deception are left wondering how people could be so blind. How do they not see that what they believe or are being taught is not in line with Scripture? Even when you show them the Bible and put that next to the lies they're being taught, they just don't see it! Why won't they change in light of the truth? Questions swirl in our minds as we wonder what to do and how to do it.

No doubt that's what Jude's readers would have been dealing with back in the first century of the church. Apostasy everywhere, with people who seemed to have made a genuine confession of faith being carried away by false doctrines. It was hard to tell who the good guys were and who should be avoided. Further, they would have seen loved ones targeted by deceivers, just like we do today.

Is there a roadmap for distinguishing when to walk with someone patiently, when to rush in and be bold, and when to put distance between ourselves and the danger? We undoubtedly need to share the truth and be on mission as Christians. The book of Jude shows us how.

The very brief book of Jude was written to condemn the practices of false teachers and encourage Christians to stand firm in the truth. Jude opens his letter explaining that he wanted to write to his recipients about their "common salvation" (Jude 3). Jude wanted to write a happy letter about all of the blessings and joys of being a Christian! Unfortunately, the gospel was under assault, so Jude changed his mind and used his letter as an occasion to tell the church it was time to contend for the faith. Isn't that something so many of us can relate to today? We'd rather talk about good things, hopeful things! Who wants to talk about all the damage the prosperity gospel is causing? It would be so much more exciting to write a book on hope or healing or Jesus' making everything okay, but there are times when we must face the hard truth. Jude had such a burden.

Some of the final verses of Jude give us instruction for focusing on growing in the truth for ourselves, and trying to reach apostates who are caught up in false gospels. Jude writes:

> But you, beloved, ought to remember the words that were spoken beforehand by the apostles of our Lord Jesus Christ, that they were saying to you, "In the last time there will be mockers, following after their own ungodly lusts." These are the ones who cause divisions, worldly-minded, devoid of the Spirit. But you, beloved, building yourselves up on your most holy faith, praying in the Holy Spirit, keep yourselves in the love of God, waiting anxiously for the mercy of our Lord Jesus Christ to eternal life. And have mercy on some, who are doubting; save others, snatching them out of the fire; and on some have mercy with fear, hating even the garment polluted by the flesh.
>
> —JUDE 17–23

Three Categories to Keep in Mind

Jude 22–23 provides us with three categories of people who are caught up in deception, along with instructions for how to interact with them. Let's look at each of them more closely.

THE DOUBTERS

Jude 22 says, "Have mercy on some, who are doubting." The doubters are the group that may challenge your patience, because you just want them to wake up and see the plain truth. Doubting (*diakrino*) gives the picture of someone wavering on the line, then partial to one side but uncertain, then in the middle but hesitant to fully cross over. Imagine the people who may drive you a little crazy because you just want them to make a decision! These are confused individuals who are vulnerable and have been manipulated by clever false teachers. Keep the door open for them. Get into their lives. Take off your shoes, stay a while, and build relationships with them for the purpose of reaching them. You don't drive by and toss a study Bible at them, saying, "Figure this out, then we can talk." You buy them a study Bible and commit to coffee meetups for however long it takes. Confess any hardheartedness you may have to the Lord, remember his mercy toward you, learn patience, ask questions, and stick with them. God has you in their lives for a reason.

THE DECEIVED

Jude 23 says that we must "save others, snatching them out of the fire." The deceived are convinced they have the truth. We are to be in rescue-operation mode with them, boldly confronting their errors and calling them to repentance. Like a Coast Guard helicopter flying into an offshore storm, we're on the lookout for those drowning in the sea of apostasy so we can drop the rope and pull them up. And if they reject the rope? We never stop praying, never stop trying, and never stop hoping they will be awakened to the danger they are in.

Jude undoubtedly understands the sovereignty of God in

saving his children and in keeping his children saved, but he's equally aware of the vessels through which God so often saves— the faithful witness of his people (Acts 1:8; Rom. 10:17). Snatching (*harpazo*) is the same word used in John 10:12 of the wolf snatching the sheep away from the hireling shepherd, and in John 10:28 of no one being able to snatch Jesus' sheep from his hand. Jude has in mind a state of readiness to rescue people.

Notice that there is no opt-out clause. No amendment because of the doctrine of election. No free pass because of God's sovereignty. No giving up because they rejected you. A true Christian is patiently yet relentlessly looking for opportunities to snatch brands from the fire.

THE DANGEROUS

Finally, Jude 23 states, "On some have mercy with fear, hating even the garment polluted by the flesh." The dangerous are those whose garments have been soiled with satanic deception. They are those who fly the flag of false doctrine with pride, convincing people with their smooth talk and flattery (Rom. 16:18). They infiltrate the highest levels of the church and undermine Christ in pulpits through their greed and heretical teaching (2 Peter 2:1–3). They are bold loyalists to apostasy, enemies of the truth, and set against Christ. With these people we are called to be merciful as well, not indifferent to the fact they have souls in need of salvation. Yet we show mercy by praying for their salvation, hoping and believing that anyone can change, all the while maintaining a fearsome devotion to our own morality. Being merciful does not mean overlooking or being a party to their dangerous beliefs.

One commentator writes, "Mercy takes into account moral distinctions. It does not treat evil as of no consequence. Christians have mercy with fear, hating even the garment spotted by the flesh."[1] What this means is we are acutely aware of where they are heading, wincing in agony for their defilement of the gospel, and calling them to repentance, but from a healthy distance.

Sometimes we're playing offense. Sometimes we're playing defense. But we must be aware that apostasy will rise in the last days (Jude 17–19; 2 Tim. 3:1–5). We need to stay rooted in our faith, hoping in the return of Christ (Jude 20–21), and we must work tirelessly to rescue those who are deceived. All along, we must trust in God's power to save his people (Rom. 1:16).

Ten Steps to Remember

In this final chapter, I want to leave you with a framework for reaching people who are caught in dangerous belief systems. I also want to share some of the ups and downs I've experienced in trying to reach family members and friends with the goal of encouraging you to know that you are not alone in your journey to reason with the deceived.

Some of the points here will stretch you; others will not be all that surprising. The reality is that God is going to use you to speak the truth to someone who needs it desperately. I hope this simple roadmap helps. It may even spark your own thoughts, so feel free to add to it, customize it, post it on your fridge, or put it in your Bible or journal. You never know when God will put you on assignment—on second thought, we're always on assignment, aren't we?

I remember when I began to have more levelheaded

---

1   George Arthur Buttrick, The Interpreter's Bible, vol. 12 (Nashville: Abingdon, 1957), 341.

heart-to-heart conversations with prosperity preaching family members. We've had more conversations than I can count over the past seven years, but they've evolved in some ways. Thinking back to when I had my eyes opened to the truth, I am certain I failed miserably at speaking the truth in love. Some of those initial discussions were tame pleadings in which I begged them to see the difference between the life we lived and what the Bible said. But some of them were Bible-thumping debates that got far too heated. Much of it was to no avail, as it seemed to be hopeless to convince them.

Instead of being patient with their blindness or showing empathy toward their indifference to the truth I was sharing, I would push harder and harder until the conversation escalated into an argument. They would call me judgmental, I'd call them blind or accuse them of being wolves in sheep's clothing, and round and round we went. This occurred during that first year of family separation until finally most of my family and I didn't speak much for the better course of one year. My father and I barely talked at all for even longer than that. My mother acted as go-between, sending the occasional text message to tell me my father loved me. Sometimes I said it back. Other times I would coldly text, "Love is seen through actions and truth. Those words are meaningless to me." So often, I neglected to respond with a tender heart. It was one of the most difficult times in my life because the gospel had divided our family and there was no template I could use to figure out how to fix it. I tried my best to trust the Lord and stick to his Word while learning how to navigate interactions with those I so ardently disagreed with.

After all of the private pleadings and intense Hinn-family confrontations, there were times when I thought all hope was

lost. Jesus' words in Matthew 10:34–38 suddenly had more meaning than ever before. Explaining that families would divide over
him, Jesus said,

> "Do not think that I came to bring peace on the earth; I did
> not come to bring peace, but a sword. For I came to set a man
> against his father, and a daughter against her mother, and a
> daughter-in-law against her mother-in-law; and a man's ene-
> mies will be the members of his household.
>
> "He who loves father or mother more than Me is not wor-
> thy of Me; and he who loves son or daughter more than Me
> is not worthy of Me. And he who does not take his cross and
> follow after Me is not worthy of Me."

The truth is right in that Scripture passage. Jesus is the dividing
line. What you do with him and the gospel he preached will determine your eternity and the eternity of those you love so dearly.
Jesus became the dividing line in our family. Some have chosen to
preach and follow the true Jesus regardless of the cost, and others
have chosen to preach and follow a false Jesus in order to get rich.
My job is to continue trying to reach them by speaking the truth
in love. Over time, some aspects of family relationships have gone
from heated debates that do not reflect Christ, to constructive discussions. Our conversations are richer and more gracious (even
when disagreeing) because there have been moments of honesty in
which certain family members admitted wrongdoing. It's not the
admission of sins that I rejoice in (though that helps) but rather the
lines of communication that open when we stop living in denial
about the past. Some things can't be changed. But the future is
hopeful if we surrender our hearts to Christ.

When will all of my family members come out from their prosperity preaching and false teachings? Will they ever? I don't know. But I've learned to focus on what I can control, and I have learned that a stand for truth doesn't have to be filled with hatred and vitriol. Showing grace and patience toward others is not condoning their behavior, but it certainly involves controlling your own. We all have to ask ourselves this important question when trying to reach people: am I trying to win the person, or am I just trying to win the argument? Your answer will reveal your heart. God is in charge of the timing. We are in charge of loving people enough to share the truth.

As promised, here is a top-ten list of things I recommend you do if you are trying to win people to the truth. I don't write this list as a self-proclaimed expert but as someone who has learned through both success and failure. Sometimes there are breakthroughs when I share the truth; sometimes there are devastating results. When I want to throw in the towel, I always go back to the Bible for motivation (1 Corinthians 13; Jude 22–23). Above all, I know Jesus can melt any heart of stone.

Keep in mind there may be times when these steps work well in chronological order, while other times you'll find yourself repeating the same steps over and over. If that's the case, you'll see why step 10 is so important.

1. PRAY FOR THEM

Charles Spurgeon rightly said, "Prayer is doubt's destroyer, ruin's remedy, the antidote to all anxieties." When we're talking about reaching friends and family, we cannot begin anywhere but prayer! Where prayer is present, hatred cannot survive. When we bow our will before God's will and ask him to work in the hearts of those we are trying to reach, it is inevitably our hearts that soften and change first. Since salvation and transformation are sovereign works of God's power, we need to pray for his power to see those things transpire. His will is that people be saved (1 Tim. 2:4), so pray for it and trust him with the results.

We should also be praying for greater faith. Conversation after conversation will occur in which people may scoff at you, or you may lovingly discuss differences only to seemingly make no progress. Do not lose heart or patience. Pray for faith.

Last, in your praying for others to stop sinning, don't forget to look in the mirror and pray that God cleanses you of your sin as well (1 John 1:9).

2. STUDY THE TRUTH

You do not need a degree in combatting false teaching to reach people—you need to be well-versed in truth. The wisdom of this world and the philosophies of man are powerless to save and transform lives, but the gospel is the "power of God" to save people (Rom. 1:16). Use that to your advantage and put the gospel in front of people as often as possible. I can't tell you how many times I have failed at this only to wind up dumbfounded over what went wrong. Looking back, I'll tell you exactly what went wrong. I was trusting in the power of my intellect and the power of my emotion (or frustration) to win a battle that only the gospel can.

Which brings up a convicting point: we need to know the gospel to share the gospel. It may seem surprising, but many Christians do not know how to effectively articulate the gospel in a conversation. Sure, we can all recite the Sunday school statement that Jesus died on the cross for our sins, but do we know the gospel well enough to spot a fake? When someone says that Jesus died to heal you and bless you on earth, do you know why that statement can be dangerous? If someone says that giving money to their ministry will give you a hundredfold blessing and heal your daughter's cancer, can you explain why that is a false promise in light of the gospel? Majoring in truth and studying sound doctrine will give you assurance as both a Christian and a witness who is trying to reach others.

One more thing I want to touch on is this: avoid hobbyhorsing on juicy gossip and the latest evangelical controversy. This doesn't mean we should avoid addressing critical issues, but as evangelicals, we can sometimes get caught up in our own drama and get distracted from our mission here on earth.

3. DEAL WITH YOUR HEART ISSUES

If you've ever wondered why people get so unhinged and angry during discussions about theology, it's usually rooted in unresolved heart issues. We can't reach others if we don't first look in the mirror to examine how we handle the process. Conflict resolution aptitude is in short supply these days. A lot of people—Christians no less—do not possess the proper disposition for healthy, robust dialogue without taking everything personally. Many have vengeful tendencies because they've never dealt with hurt, anger, or fear in biblically healthy ways. I say this with love. If you have trouble agreeing with this list, you probably have a heart issue in this area. By that I mean your pride is keeping you from seeing your blind spot when it comes to loving others, controlling your emotions, and managing disagreement in a God-honoring way. And it takes one to know one! I have been there, and the struggle is real. I failed numerous times and said plenty of emotionally driven things toward my false-teaching family. It got us nowhere but into a war of words.

Before I ever said anything publicly (like in a blog, book, or video) about the prosperity gospel, systems were put in place for my own good. My pastor held me accountable by requiring me to submit prayer reports about my prayer life for a season, I saturated my life with Scripture, and I was in counseling of various kinds over the course of three years. Counseling and personal mentorship were nonnegotiable. Some people may scoff at counseling or therapy, but I am so thankful for the people the Lord used to help provide wisdom I had never heard before. All of my counselors—who were either pastors, retired pastors, or Christian leaders with long resumes of faithful mentorship—said similar things about the importance of speaking the hard truth in love while maintaining a healthy attitude.

Spend some time counseling your emotions, resisting the urge to explode during your cage stage, and ask yourself, "Do I just want blood because I am contentious? Or do I genuinely have a heart for this individual?"

4. SEEK A PRIVATE AUDIENCE

Maybe you have, but I have never won someone to the truth or seen God open the eyes of a spiritually blind person by exploding on them via Twitter or Facebook. Also, belittling the beliefs of others in a group setting will only breed conflict and insecurity and likely lead to a war of words. Last, who hasn't seen the uselessness of debating over text messages? Again, I've tried that route and failed miserably. Try writing a heartfelt letter with an invitation to meet privately, or make a phone call and invite the individual to share a meal and catch up on things. Seeking a private audience should be viewed as a bridge-building strategy, not a one-and-done mic drop so you can serve them up a monologue entree of your opinion.

You may even consider—get ready to be blown away by my wisdom here—pursuing a friendship or relationship with someone you disagree with! Isn't that profound? You're likely picking up my sarcasm. I don't mean to be rude, but seriously, we need to do better at building relational bridges with people if we are going to reach their hearts. I meet people all the time who do what I call drive-by evangelism. They take shots at people in conversations, then keep on passing through, never to stop and spend time in a two-way discussion with the person they're attacking.

Here's a cliche that has stood the test of time: "People don't care how much you know until they know how much you care." You're better off focusing on loving the person by relating with them in a personal way than by engaging them in debate. Without meaningful, personal interaction, we will fail to reach people who are caught up in deception. Remember, relationships are all about people!

5. ASK QUESTIONS

My friend Wyatt recently expressed his frustration because he was unable to get through to one of his friends who was caught up in some seriously deceptive stuff. Take the prosperity gospel and multiply it by ten—that's what his friend was into. Together we brainstormed about his approach. Up to that point, he was having a hard time holding in his reactions to her viewpoints. It was making for some serious tension in the friendship, so after some discussion, we agreed it was best for him to try asking questions in a genuine way so he could show more understanding than he had done previously.

The results? Astounding. Within a week, he came up to me at church exclaiming, "Dude!" (We're in California.) "It totally worked! I asked questions, listened to her responses, and sought to understand her point of view before sharing my thoughts in a fair way. It was the best conversation we've ever had, and she didn't feel like I was attacking her."

Wyatt's approach changed the minute he started using a little strategy called HMU. HMU stands for "help me understand." You have to admit, it's bound to work better than questions like, "Why in the world would you believe in that ridiculousness?" When we ask genuine questions in an effort to understand the person, it shows we care. This allows us to have a more fruitful discussion and preserve the relationship for future conversation. If you're trying to reach someone, they need to know you understand them. Understanding doesn't mean you are agreeing with them or condoning any behaviors you oppose. It is simply a mark of your maturity and self-control when you can manage your emotions enough to understand someone you differ with.

6. SPEAK THE TRUTH IN LOVE

Paul says we need to be "speaking the truth in love" (Eph. 4:15). This is one of the hardest things to do. It's easy to be nasty with people we don't agree with! Loving people we don't agree with is hard, humbling work. Speaking the truth in love means being truthful, accurate, fair, patient, gentle, humble, and consistent. We need to remember that if we play offense, people will naturally play defense. Speaking the truth in love is going to involve a hard conversation already; why make it harder by being abrasive? In a loving conversation, there shouldn't be an axe to grind. That doesn't mean you have to compromise the truth either. If disagreement occurs (which is more than likely), keep step 7 front and center in your mind.

7. DON'T PERSONALIZE DISAGREEMENT

I've been told time and again by older, wiser pastors, "Don't personalize disagreement." It's sound wisdom that rings true no matter what kind of conflict you're facing. Remember, as much as we should all own the Great Commission and share the truth, we don't own that truth. It's God's truth—we're merely the ambassadors conveying his message.

If someone is scoffing at your loving words of truth, don't take it personally—they're scoffing at God. When we get bent out of shape and react as though people are rejecting us, we're operating under a bit of a god complex. We aren't God, so we need not act like people are disrespecting us when they turn their backs on truth. Just like we are managers of our children (and are not their God) and train their hearts to obey God, trust God, and look to God, we are also managers of the other relationships in our lives, and we should look at those relationships as opportunities to reflect God's heart to people. On judgment day, people aren't going to answer to you and me. They will face the Lord. We need to keep that in mind and not personalize disagreement.

8. LEAVE THE DOOR OPEN

Take a deep breath for a moment and then let's face the music on this one together. We have all made the fateful mistake of giving the ultimatum, "If you don't change, I'm cutting you out of my life!" Guilty as charged. The lesson we learn from this sort of remark is that shutting the door on people and burning bridges is only for a short list of reasons. Abuse is no doubt a good one.

Violence is as well. But if we're theologically disagreeing on something, is it necessary to go to such an extreme?

I propose we slow down and ask some important questions. First, is this person a dangerous false teacher who should be refuted and kept at arm's length, or is this just Aunt Matilda trying to convince us to believe in speaking in tongues? The Bible gives credence to cutting off those who are dangerous and deceptive, but not everybody fits in that category.

Second, is this a disagreement so divisive that no relationship is possible, or is it our pride that tries to turn every Thanksgiving dinner into a theological debate? Sometimes, the people in our lives just want to have a normal discussion and be treated like people, not opponents being beaten down. Leaving the door open for levelheaded dialogue doesn't mean we are agreeing with or even overlooking their beliefs.

Finally, answer this series of questions: If you were on the other end of your own words, how would you respond? Does the punishment you're dishing out fit the crime? Is it possible that you're missing out on the purpose of evangelism and the joy of reaching people you love because you keep slamming the door shut on them? If we want to be the first phone call people make when they hit rock bottom or have a genuine question about the truth, we need to leave the door open, keep the conversation warm, and be ready to brew a pot of coffee.

9. PROVIDE RESOURCES

When, not if, you're doing steps 1–8 and someone comes to you with a changed heart and mind, you'd better be ready. This is when things get fun! Do you remember when you came to know the truth about something and you stayed up until 2:00 a.m.

researching on YouTube, ordering books, and staring at the ceiling trying to make sense of it all? I do. That is exactly what your friends and family will be going through when you reach them with the truth. They're going to need clear next steps that they should take.

Make a list of churches you trust, doctrines that helped you grow, books that changed your life, and pastors who are reliable. Solid Bible teachers without moral scandal or compromised beliefs are in short supply these days, but they do exist. Many people coming out of deceptive circumstances are desperately looking for someone they can trust. Help them. It's vitally important to do more than just pat someone on the back and say, "I'm glad you're out now. Good luck!" We need to invite them to our discipleship small group, meet with them for a season if possible, and let them know the hours we are available.

Finally, I have met more people than I can count who have needed (and benefited from) counseling after spending years trapped in abusive, deceptive prosperity gospel churches. Where your counsel falls short, send them to certified Bible counselors.

10. NEVER GIVE UP

No matter how dark the day seems or how lost people are, believers are never to give up on them. Yes, God is sovereign over salvation, and he is the one who awakens the dead sinner's heart to his love, but that doesn't negate our role as ambassadors fulfilling the Great Commission (2 Cor. 5:21; Matt. 28:16–20). Love never gives up—period. One of the most powerful statements ever made about love is found in 1 Corinthians 13:4–7: "Love is patient, love is kind and is not jealous; love does not brag and is not arrogant, does not act unbecomingly; it does not seek its own, is not provoked, does not take into account a wrong suffered, does not rejoice in unrighteousness, but rejoices with the truth; bears all things, believes all things, hopes all things, endures all things."

Loving people and never giving up still includes standing boldly for the truth and not rejoicing in unrighteousness, but it is balanced with bearing, believing, hoping, and enduring in all things. What a challenging, life-altering perspective!

Isn't it humbling to imagine the patience and grace that God has shown to us? How can we do anything but respond with patience and grace toward others? Peter describes God's patience with us when he writes, "The Lord is not slow about His promise, as some count slowness, but is patient toward you, not wishing for any to perish but for all to come to repentance" (2 Peter 3:9). That care for the human soul should come through in the way we reach others, hoping and praying for a thief-on-the-cross moment to happen to any of our friends or loved ones. It's never too late for anyone to repent of their sins and turn to Jesus Christ as Lord and Savior. Pride will tell you to give up, but you need to tell pride where to go. We never give up on lost and deceived souls.

Where Do We Go from Here?

As this final chapter comes to a close, I want to ask you an honest question: What are you going to do about what you have learned? Maybe God has given you some influence in this world and you've been waiting for the right moment to use it. Perhaps you have been blindly following prosperity preachers, and this book helped you see the empty promises for what they really are. Or it could be that you're a believer enjoying the safety and security of a solid church led by trustworthy pastors. Perhaps it's time to leave your comfort zone and step out in faith to seek the lost, trusting that God will use you in his sovereign plan.

Who will you reach with the saving gospel of Jesus?

And have mercy on some, who are doubting; save others, snatching them out of the fire; and on some have mercy with fear, hating even the garment polluted by the flesh.

—JUDE 22–23

Frequently Asked Questions

Like every story, and like every book, it's just not necessary to give some details. I've tried to give you all I can to help you understand what the power of the true gospel can do. That being said, here are the questions most people ask after I share my story with them. I trust this will help you.

What are things like with your family now?

A mixture of victories and challenges. Some family members have been walking in the truth, while others remain convinced that their theological positions and behaviors are justified by their special anointing. From time to time, I receive phone calls from family members who are inspired and encouraged by the truth, and sometimes I receive warnings to stop what I am doing for fear of divine judgment. Overall, there have been honest conversations that seem to make progress, and setbacks that come when certain behaviors and abuses are repeated. There are things that are not yet fully clear, and that keeps me humbly trusting the Lord. We pray for my family often.

After seeing all the fake healings and deception within your uncle's ministry, do you still believe God heals people and can do miracles?

Absolutely. I restate this time and time again, but it still remains one of the top questions people ask. I unequivocally believe God is a healer and can heal anyone at any time. I also believe that he still does miracles today. That being said, I don't believe that anyone is going around doing miracles (or creating "atmospheres" for real miracles like my uncle claims) today exactly like Jesus did. No one holds the power to heal people at will. Though there are many who have copied the tactics of healing evangelists, they are mostly just new faces playing the old game. If they do have the power to heal people, they'd be making headlines by clearing out hospitals with their healing powers. When people are sick, I believe we should pray for healing and endure trials in faith. No matter the outcome, we ought to pray to the Father like Jesus did in Luke 22:42, when he said, "Not my will but yours be done."

Why were you hired as a youth pastor when the church knew you came out of a prosperity gospel background?

This is the number one question I get after inquiries about family relationships. Long story short, our church was called Moment Church back then, and it was one of those trendy church plants built on the seeker-driven model. We brought in big names to draw crowds, put on a good show, played to people's emotions, and gave some gospel along the way. We were by no means a "dangerous" church, but our trajectory was off target. Over a six-month period, God transformed many of us. We went from being loyal to old beliefs and methods to being loyal to Scripture. God did incredible things in the hearts of the teaching pastor and the team. We received some help from faithful Bible teachers, read some books on biblical church models, and focused on being a biblical church ourselves. The result? An eventual name change to Mission Bible Church, the exit of many people who were not on board with the new vision, and surging growth both spiritually and numerically after that—the most important being the spiritual growth. That's where we are today. Thankfully, the Lord used the avenue he did to get me out, and he matured our church beyond those early years as well. We often say, "It's all grace!"

Why do you feel it was necessary to write a book? Shouldn't this all be kept private since it is a personal matter?

That is a fair question, and one that many pastors may answer in different ways. My take on this is both methodological and theological. From a methodological standpoint, I chose to share my testimony because God uses testimonies to spread the gospel, inspire others, and glorify himself. In the New Testament, we see many testimonies that serve as illustrations of what God can do. The Bible is packed with the testimonies and stories of people—from Ruth to Zaccheus (Luke 19:1–10) to Paul the apostle (Acts 9:1–19)—who were transformed by the truth and turned to worship the one true God.

Though not on the same level as the Bible, modern testimonies are trophies of God's power. They point people to him as the solution to man's problem of sin. I chose to share my testimony through book form because I love to write.

Theologically speaking, based on the biblical standard of repentance and the biblical standard for pastoral ministry, silence is not an option for anyone claiming the title of pastor. We are not only called to show the fruits of repentance in coming clean (Matt. 3:8), but as pastors we are to preach and teach what is true and refute what is false (2 Tim. 4:1–5).

In addition, I didn't set out to write a book—it just happened over time. Much was said in private over the years, then some people asked questions in our church and in our Christian community, then I began blogging about the topics surrounding the issue to safeguard people in my church and help people like me, then the testimony was shared, then a publisher asked if I would write a book to showcase God's power in saving people and to point people to the truth. I accepted the opportunity and plan to use every ounce of energy, publicity, and any notoriety on this issue to make Jesus famous and preach the true gospel. That's what every Christian, regardless of their last name, is called to do.

Who cares if a prosperity preacher drives a fancy car or lives in a mansion? What about all of the humanitarian work they do for orphans and the money they give to the poor?

At best, this is merely a civil virtue. Many dishonest people still do some good things. It doesn't negate their heinous acts (unless repented of). Prosperity gospel ministries pull in tens (in many cases hundreds) of millions of dollars per year. It's a common public relations strategy to be philanthropic while at the same time pocketing large sums of money. Many corporations and individuals do that, but prosperity preachers are building their wealth on deception. It's like stealing ten dollars from a helpless child's piggy bank without his knowing it, then giving him a dollar as though it were a generous gift. Here's the process broken down into simple steps:

1. Designate a percentage of ministry income to sponsor orphans, build an orphanage, or support the marginalized and broken of our society. Document it well and make sure people know about all of the humanitarian work you do.
2. Live a lavish lifestyle on the rest of your donor support, purchasing luxury cars, multi-million-dollar homes, private planes, rare jewels, etc.
3. When the church or the general public questions your love of money, lavish lifestyle, or outlandish behavior as a pastor, point to step 1.
4. Repeat.

I don't think it's wise to weigh people's integrity by how much humanitarian work they do. We can all think of numerous examples of people who were abusing their power to exploit others and get rich while shaking hands and kissing babies for the cameras. It's best to look at someone's teaching in light of what the Bible says. That's the measuring stick we all must stand next to.

What do you say to people who think you're just trading on the family name to get rich and famous?

Questions like this are usually based on the presumption that fame is the goal, or on the false premise that I am using my uncle's name to make a name for myself.

First, Proverbs 22:1 says, "A good name is to be more

desired than great wealth." When you think about trading on the family name, there isn't much to trade on. My uncle has systematically exploited poverty-stricken countries for forty years to get rich, and now other family members are following in his footsteps. Allow me to get painfully honest for a moment: for most of our family members, it can be pretty embarrassing to be a Hinn. Many of us would prefer to be unknown, hardworking, honest people who die in obscurity having loved others and served God.

Second, I am not famous and don't want to be rich. I am nothing but a person who was transformed by the power of the true gospel. Because of my last name, my story of being a pastor became interesting for people and created a sphere of influence, but I am just another ambassador for Christ taking his message to those I can reach. Whether my sphere of influence is two people or two million, I'm still going to do what people did in the Bible and testify of what God has done. "Trying to get famous" grossly misses the point of proclaiming the gospel. Fame is fleeting and money creates a false sense of security. I lived that life already. It's a house of cards.

Like any Christian, I want to live for the glory of God and use my gifts, talents, resources, and testimony to point others to him. There is one kingdom I want to see built, one king I want to serve, and one name I want to make famous. Jesus is my motivation. One of the scariest realities is that he will judge my motives and my works one day (2 Cor. 5:10). We all have a name that we didn't choose, and we all have one life to live. How we live on earth impacts our eternity. One day, I hope my gravestone simply says, "Loved his wife, loved his children, loved the church, and lived for Christ."

Where can people find more of your teaching as a follow-up to this book?

I host a resource site that offers mostly free material (except books, since publishers sell those). You can go to www.forthegospel. org for equipping tools like blog articles, teaching video, sermons, podcasts, and books. I'm also active on Facebook and Twitter (@costiwhinn for both).

APPENDIX 2

Recommended Reading

Here are some resources that over the last several years have helped me find answers to the questions and the confusion brought about by my former false beliefs. Though this list is hardly exhaustive, I trust it will serve as a kickstarter for those who are looking for answers. I'll continue to recommended resources on social media and at *www.forthegospel.org*.

Books that expose prosperity theology and associated movements:

Prosperity? Seeking the True Gospel by Ken Mbugua and Michael Maura

Health, Wealth, and Happiness by David W. Jones and Russell S. Woodbridge

Strange Fire by John MacArthur

Clouds without Water II by Justin Peters (DVD)
Defining Deception by Costi W. Hinn and Anthony Wood
The Confusing World of Benny Hinn by G. Richard Fisher and M. Kurt
    Goedelman

Books that explain the historical roots of prosperity theology:
Blessed by Kate Bowler
The History of New Thought: From Mind Cure to Positive Thinking and
    the Prosperity Gospel by John S. Haller Jr. and Robert C. Fuller

Books that will help you understand sovereignty, suffering, joy, trials, and evil:
If God Is Good: Faith in the Midst of Suffering and Evil by Randy Alcorn
A Place of Healing: Wrestling with the Mysteries of Suffering, Pain, and
    God's Sovereignty by Joni Eareckson Tada
Choosing Gratitude by Nancy Leigh DeMoss
The Invisible Hand: Do All Things Really Work for Good? by R. C. Sproul

Books that will help you understand the biblical nature of God:
The Holy Spirit in Today's World by W. A. Criswell
God the Son Incarnate: The Doctrine of Christ by Stephen J. Wellum
The Attributes of God by A. W. Pink

Books that will help you understand God's will on healing:
The Healing Promise: Is It Always God's Will to Heal? by Richard
    Mayhue

Books that will help you understand wealth and stewardship:
Master Your Money by Ron Blue
Managing God's Money by Randy Alcorn

Financial Peace University by Dave Ramsey (includes DVDs)
Living with Wealth without Losing Your Soul by Steve Perry

Books that will inspire you to stand boldly in the truth:

Warnings to the Churches by J. C. Ryle

The Truth War by John MacArthur

Church Awakening by Charles R. Swindoll

Stand: A Call for the Endurance of the Saints edited by John Piper and
    Justin Taylor

We Cannot Stay Silent by Albert Mohler

Books that will help you find a biblical church and understand the gospel:

Nine Marks of a Healthy Church by Mark Dever

The Master's Plan for the Church by John MacArthur

Conversion by Michael Lawrence

The Gospel by Ray Ortlund

Visual Theology by Tim Challies and Josh Byers

Books that will help you interpret the Bible faithfully:

Grasping God's Word by J. Scott Duvall and J. Daniel Hays

Basic Bible Interpretation by Roy B. Zuck